EARLY VILLAGES OF STAMFORD, CONNECTICUT

The Cove and Long Ridge

Jeanne Majdalany

HERITAGE BOOKS
2015

HERITAGE BOOKS

AN IMPRINT OF HERITAGE BOOKS, INC.

Books, CDs, and more—Worldwide

For our listing of thousands of titles see our website
at
www.HeritageBooks.com

Published 2015 by
HERITAGE BOOKS, INC.
Publishing Division
5810 Ruatan Street
Berwyn Heights, Md. 20740

Heritage Books by Jeanne Majdalany:

Early Villages of Stamford, Connecticut: The Cove and Long Ridge

Poems on Stone in Stamford, Connecticut
Jeanne Majdalany and Jean Mulkerin

Story of the Early Settlers of Stamford, Connecticut, 1641–1700,
Including Genealogies of Principal Families
History by Jeanne Majdalany, Genealogies by
Edith M. Wicks and Jeanne Majdalany

Cover illustration: Section of the pencil sketch of
John William Holly's Island made in 1842 by Burfield(?)

Library of Congress No. 79-63008

International Standard Book Numbers
Paperbound: 978-0-7884-0893-9
Clothbound: 978-0-7884-6133-0

Acknowledgments

It is hard to express an appropriate thank-you to the many people who gave generously of their time and of their memories and so helped to produce this little book. Those who have lived in the Cove area were particularly helpful: Mrs. Clara Dippel, Mrs. Edith Murray, Mr. Gerald Rybnick, Mr. Frank Daley, and Mr. Thomas Purcell gave me so many little stories and facts that I was unable to include in a history of this sort all that I wanted to. Another little history should be written about the Cove residents alone.

My special thanks go to Mr. William Skiddy Payson, without whose very generous assistance this book could not have been written, for the Minute Books for the Stamford Manufacturing Company, which he lent me, are invaluable. Also, his many stories of the Skiddys created a colorful picture of the great period of the mills.

Miss Elizabeth Sumner, a Holly descendant who lives in California, has been constantly in touch sending pictures, letters, and much encouragement.

Mr. Ronald Marcus has given two forms of assistance: he found the early laws and acts of Connecticut for me as well as other recondite bits of information, and he has read my work, giving most useful criticism at several points.

Mrs. Lois Dater and Mr. Robert Halliday have been most helpful in finding photographs and offering technical, and often time-consuming, assistance throughout.

Others who have offered encouragement and suggestion are Mrs. Virginia Davis and Mrs. Jean Mulkerin.

Those who work in an official capacity at the Stamford Town Hall, the Ferguson Library, the Park Department, and the Stamford Historical Society have been generous with their help also.

Mr. Kurt Blumberg has been unsparing in his firm support and his enthusiasm. The Stamford Historical Society and I both thank him deeply for securing the necessary financial support.

Further acknowledgments may be seen attached to the bibliography at the end of this book. To all I say thank you.

...l sketch of John William Holly's Island made in 1842 by Burfield (?). The scene is ...lge to the west of the Cove. Note the dam, East Mill, Holly Mansion, and West ...

Courtesy of Miss ...

Table of Contents

Introduction

THE HISTORY OF
THE COVE IN STAMFORD, CONNECTICUT

INTRODUCTION

Along the Connecticut shore of Long Island Sound, just at the boundary line between Stamford and Darien, there has grown up in recent years an extensive playground where the inhabitants of Stamford may enjoy their leisure hours. There was a time in the 1950's when Stamford, through negligence, almost lost control of this attractive area; belatedly, a sudden resolve gave rise to popular demand for rescuing the site from the Connecticut Light and Power Company at the cost of $485,000.[1] Since that time it has been developed slowly and with care. Today there are tennis courts, an ice rink, and a boat marina on the mainland, and on what is now called Cove Island there are open spaces for ball games and kite flying, picnic areas scattered among the locusts and maple trees, and two lovely beaches known as East Beach and Horseshoe Beach, which are backed by tasteful pavilions containing only essential facilities. This last summer a new attraction was added; rowboats were made available so that one could lazily explore the reaches of Holly Pond to the north of the island.

In the summer the parking lot adjacent to the bridge over to the island is often filled to capacity, but the Cove area is large enough so that one experiences the happy spirit of fun and relaxation. In the winter a lonely walk along the beach with the wind blowing stiff and fresh gives a sense of being far from any city. A stroll to Pound Rocks, a promontory on the southeast tip, is rewarded by a glorious view: nearby are wheeling seagulls and little jagged-edged islands, and across the Sound, its waters dotted often with ships and boats, lies the soft shore of Long Island.

Holly Pond to the north of the island is a comparatively quiet spot, but it has not always been so. Once this was Noroton Harbor where sailing ships rode the waters and tied up near the mouth of the Noroton River. For example, in 1688 a shipbuilder

1

named George Phillips sold to David Weed and others "the good Briggandine called the friends Adventure" "now riding in Norrowton River."[2] It weighed seventy-six tons and was a two-masted sailing vessel.

The boundary line between Stamford and Darien cuts roughly from the mouth of the pond slightly west of true north to the mouth of the Noroton River, which it then follows. Across the Noroton River near its mouth runs the main road between Stamford and Darien, the Boston Post Road, or the Country Road as it was called in Stamford's early days. At that time the two towns were not divided, Darien breaking away in 1820.

What makes Holly Pond a pond rather than a harbor is that its mouth is actually a "gut" or narrow passage between Brush Island on the Darien side and Cove Island on the Stamford side. A dam across this gut served to cut it off still more so that it became a millpond. Brush Island is now incorporated into the whole Noroton peninsula, once known as Noroton Neck, and Cove Island, previously a part of the mainland, is now an actual island with a smaller, man-made gut on its northwestern side. Today the southern part of this smaller body of water on the west of the island (Bishop's Cove in the old days) forms a harbor where many of Stamford's small pleasure craft are moored.

CHAPTER ONE

THE COVE AREA FROM
1641 TO 1790

When Stamford began its history in 1641, the settlers preferred to dwell near the center of the settlement and, as it grew, along the coastline and by the rivers. Families such as Jonas Weed's and the Waterburys are to be found living near the Noroton River along the Country Road in the middle 1600's. They also spread out into the northern portions of Noroton Neck. The river was recognized as a good source of power for a sawmill, and one was built there to be of service to the little Noroton community as early as 1696.[1]

The western side of Cove Pond was not settled at all, for the northern part was Noroton Hill, and south of the hill itself the primarily flat open land was seen as excellent for common agricultural use and so was set apart as the East Field, later Eastfield. There were four common fields that the first settlers marked out; East Field, according to Stamford's historian Dr. Feinstein, had twenty-two owners and was divided into at least fifty-three strips in 1650.[2] It covered the area between the swamp on the east side of Shippan and the Cove. The northern boundary, according to a map drawn by Judge H. Stanley Finch,[3] was on a line with the south end of Weed Circle (once Waterbury's Island) and the tract lay south presumably to where the rocks, salt meadows, and small water inlets made the land useless. Although the owners had their rights in the fields and were responsible for their portions of the fence, the town government could reserve a field for the cultivation of a common staple; for example, in 1680 the town decided that the East Field should be planted with winter corn.[4] Towards the end of the century private ownership took over, and by 1703 Eastfield was closed. The area continued to be called by that name in the land deeds for the next century.

On May 22, 1666 it is recorded that "every man did by vote surrender up all their right they had in the land lying on the other side of the long swamp in the east field to make a horse pasture,"[5] and the stipulation was made that there should be no mares in it. The area was to be fenced by "a three-rail fence beginning at long swamp," and it was to run "straight to the east side of the land." The fence was to be made "by any horsekeepers who shall have liberty to fence on one horse or two." The fence was marked out, the fifty-six names of those owning horses listed, and a viewer was appointed for the horse-pasture the following spring.[6] In 1680 a cartway was to be made "into ye horsepasture"[7]; this, naturally enough, became known as Horsepasture Road, and today it is known as Cove Road. The horsepasture was broken up ten years later,[8] but again the old name hung on for many years.

An interesting adjunct to the horsepasture was the pound, a place that was designated by the town government for enclosing straying animals. A pounder was appointed each year. It seems that animals often got loose, for fences weren't well kept up by the owners. The animals were impounded and the owners had to pay a fine (one shilling in 1671 and five shillings in 1673)[9], much as is still in force today for dogs, in particular. The pound was located on the peninsula (which today is Cove Island) to the east of the horsepasture proper.

In 1676/77 the decision was made in the town meeting to lay out the horsepasture to private ownership, at which time four men received small portions of the pound land.[10] Soon these portions began to change hands. The first land deed that is recorded in the Stamford Land Records on the pound land is to be found in Book A, page 101, where Cornelios Jons in 1681 is recorded as selling to "Nicolus Webster" 3 acres of the pound of the horsepasture, which land was bounded on the east by the cove and on the west by town land or a cartway.[11] Two months later John Slawson also sold "Nicoless Webster" a portion of "upland in ye pound in ye horsepasture,"[11] and a half year later Webster bought two adjoining pieces from Henery Smith.[12] He now owned all the eastern side of the peninsula, bounded by "ye pound-gutt" on the east, the water on the south, "the highway [read cartway!] down to the rocks" on the west, and a small bit of land belonging to Sam Fitch on the north;[13] Fitch's piece later came to Webster also.[14] He now owned a total of 10¼ acres or a little less than half the peninsula. Nicholas' two sons sold it all to Sergeant David Waterbury in 1696 and 1699.[15] Sergeant David had also bought by public outcry, as recorded of

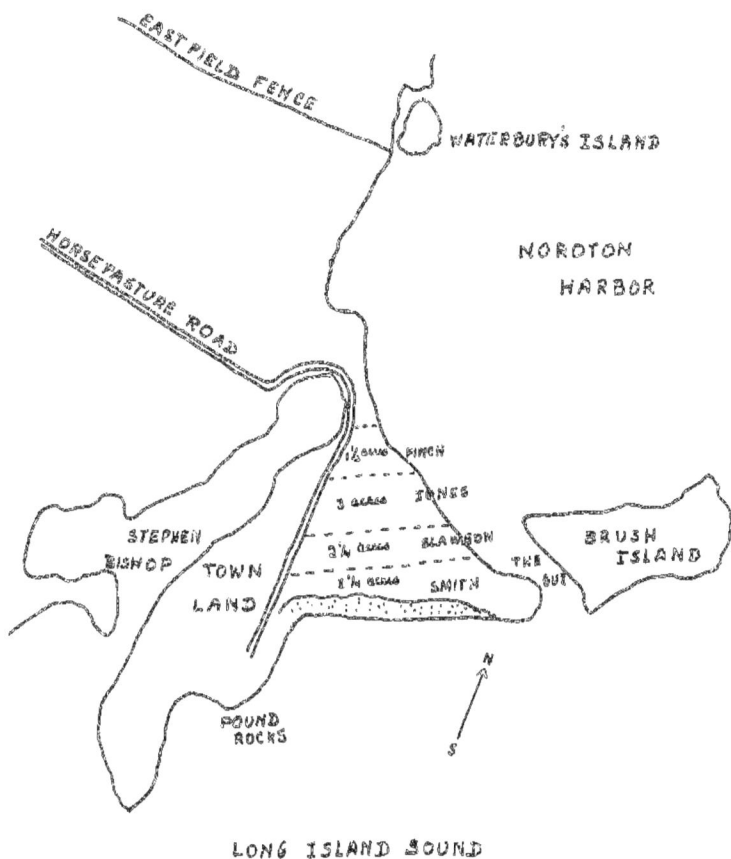

EAST FIELD FENCE

WATERBURY'S ISLAND

NOROTON HARBOR

HORSE PASTURE ROAD

1¼ acres FINCH

3 acres JONES

2½ acres SLAWSON

2½ acres SMITH

STEPHEN BISHOP

TOWN LAND

BRUSH ISLAND

THE GUT

N

S

POUND ROCKS

LONG ISLAND SOUND

THE POUND IN THE 1680'S

A SKETCH MAP SHOWING APPROXIMATE LAND BOUNDS

J. Majdalany

5

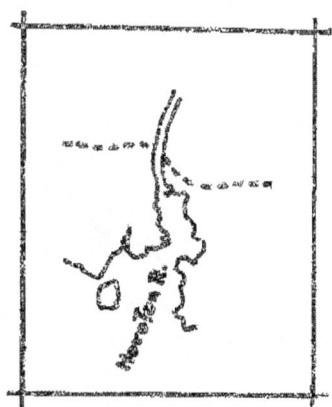

THE COVE AREA c.1775

Part of a map in the Clinton Collection,
William Clements Library, Ann Arbor,
Michigan. Courtesy of the Stamford Historical
Society.

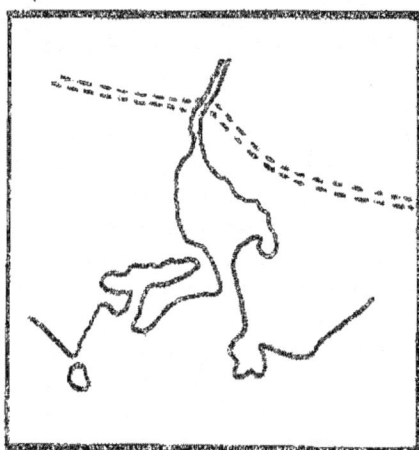

THE COVE AREA

Part of a map drawn in the late eighteenth
century, once owned by Harriet Davenport
and given to the Stamford Historical Society
by Mr. Lurelle Gould.

the town meeting of December 19, 1696, "all ye town land upon the pound" for the price of "six pounds, twenty shillings and seven pence."[16] It is unfortunate that the acreage isn't given, but by deduction, since later deeds refer to the island as having about 29 acres, we can judge the town land to have been about 18 acres.

One regulation about the pound appeared just previous to David Waterbury's acquisition. It was to be fenced in "for a close for to improve for corn and there [was] to be allowed a highway down to the pound gate and a payer [pair] of bars to ye highway."[17] David probably had his eye on this choice piece since he already had a good deal of meadow land to the north and west and was clearly accruing a sizeable estate. In 1688 he acquired a little island next to his expanse of meadow.[18] This island, now Weed Circle, was known for many years as Waterbury's Island. To the north of it was a little cove and to the west, salt marshes, which later were filled in, making the island a part of the mainland.

On the west of Sergeant David Waterbury's new acquisition of pound land was Bishop's Cove. Bishop's Cove received its name from Stephen Bishop, who desired to buy the cove "at the mouth of the pound" in 1686 and was granted permission by the town.[19] At that time the cove ran roughly north and south unimpeded by any bridge (there are two today) up to where the pound joined the mainland (now cut through) by the millpond. In 1710 Stephen sold the northern half of Bishop's Cove to Thomas Talmadge, a weaver.[20] One wonders how they used it — perhaps for its produce. Both here and in the millpond oyster beds were extensive; also sedge was valuable. The two men, whatever use they made of it, kept their partnership of the cove, but after their deaths the grandson of Stephen sold his half to John Petit.[21]

David Waterbury's ownership of the pound passed on to Jonas Weed "of Noroton Corners."[22] Jonas was the fourth of fourteen or so Jonases of Stamford, and he had married Sarah Waterbury, Sergeant (later Lieutenant) David's daughter. Jonas left the pound in his will to his seventh son Gideon in 1753,[23] and in 1767 Gideon bought the whole of Bishop's Cove from its other owners.[24] When he died in 1784, he had no immediate heirs, and so his estate was divided among his eight sisters and brothers or their heirs, as only three of them were still alive.[25] One can have slight contact with this gentleman today by visiting the very overgrown graveyard southeast of the Halfway House Restaurant and standing before his rather crude, handcut tombstone inscribed "Gideon Weid" beneath a childish-looking angel head.

The pound was divided between Gideon's brother Silvanus and his sister Sarah Bishop, later Hait or Hoyt, but it all became Jonas Weed, Jr.'s (the son of Sylvanus) by 1790.[26] Jonas also bought from his cousin John Weed six acres at the mouth of the pound, which was called "the close", and which had descended from John's grandfather Jonas of Noroton Corners to his father Lieutenant Hezekiah and hence to him.[27]

In all of the land dealings up to 1790 there is never a building mentioned in the whole of this area west of Noroton Cove except, of course, along the Country Road on Noroton Hill. Beginning, however, with the 1790's a dramatic change took place, and the two men responsible for it were John William Holly and William Fitch.

In Memory of
Mr Gideon Weid Who
Depart'd this Life Apl 25 A D
1784 in the 68th year of his Age

8

CHAPTER TWO
THE COVE AREA IN THE TIME OF
JOHN WILLIAM HOLLY
1791-1838

John William Holly was a fifth-generation Holly in the direct line from John Holly, who was one of the leaders among the early settlers of Stamford. This first John Holly's second son was Captain Increase, whose oldest son was known as John Holly, cooper (or barrel maker). John Holly, cooper's oldest son John gained the title of ensign as he fought in the French and Indian Wars, and he too named his first son John. It was this John who was the father of John William Holly. Unfortunately, he became an officer in the British Royal Navy at the time of the American Revolution, and in 1778 he sailed forth on a mission from which he never returned.[1]

Prior to his father's departure young John William had been placed under the protection of the British, and he lived in New York City and at Lloyds Neck on Long Island until 1782 when at age twenty he returned to Stamford.[2] He applied to the State of Connecticut praying "pardon . . . for joining the enemy and living under their protection" and asking "liberty to reside in this State." This permission seems to have been readily granted.[3]

John William's grandfather, Ensign John, must have been largely responsible for his only son's family, and when he died five years later, in 1787, he left John William and his brother David each a house and lands.[4] John William's house was on Elm Street near the old school (not far from St. John's Square), and when he married Rebecca Welles, the Reverend Noah Welles' daughter, in 1787, they set up housekeeping there. John William, incidentally, was a member of good standing of St. John's Episcopal Church at least as early as 1784.

William Fitch was John William Holly's brother-in-law. He was six years older than John William and had married Elizabeth, John William's younger sister, in 1781. The two Hollys, John William and David, worked with William Fitch at his mill on Mill River.[5] The tax lists from 1786 to 1789 refer to William Fitch as a miller. By 1791 William Fitch and John William Holly (who had recently decided to set up a cloth factory)[6] evidently felt well enough established and also knowledgeable enough to try a new venture, and so William Fitch, having carefully considered the whole pound peninsula and having noted the points of land on it, bought from Jonas Weed, Jr. three separate acres. One was on the neck of the pound with Bishop's Cove to the west of it and "Noroton Harbour" to the east; one was on the southwest corner at the outlet of Bishop's Cove; and the last was on the southeast corner with Noroton Gut to the north and east.[7]

Then at the August 18th town meeting William Fitch presented a petition for permission to put up a mill dam across Noroton Gut. He maintained that the mill would be built within the next seven years and that he would grind and bolt [to bolt is to pass through a sieve] for the inhabitants...at said mill for the same toll that the other mills in said town levy...." He also agreed that after the dam had been shut three years, he would once every summer open it and draw off the water, "giving notice to the inhabitants" so that they would have "an opportunity to take the shellfish therein." He would "at all times keep a good scow in the millpond sufficient to carry six hundred bushels of grain." He also agreed to build a wharf for free use and to settle any claims for damages this work might cause. A special meeting on August 22nd voted unanimously to grant Fitch the right to go ahead. He also received a patent from the State of Connecticut.[8]

In November of the same year, 1791, John William Holly bought four and a half acres right across the northern part of the pound peninsula; this was bounded on the northwest by Fitch's acre there. (See early 1790's map.) The old driftroad or cartway still existed through the neck and through this land and south through Jonas Weed's land.[9]

The dam and the grist mill were not built on Fitch's land after all but on John William Holly's at a point directly across from the northern part of Brush Island. There is a statement in a news clipping affixed to the Holly Genealogy to the effect that John William was a staunch Tory in spirit, and this fact caused difficulties in his getting rights to build a dam and mill.[10] It does seem more logical, though, that Fitch should have taken the leadership position since he was the older man and had owned a mill previously. In any case, work went ahead, and soon two

10

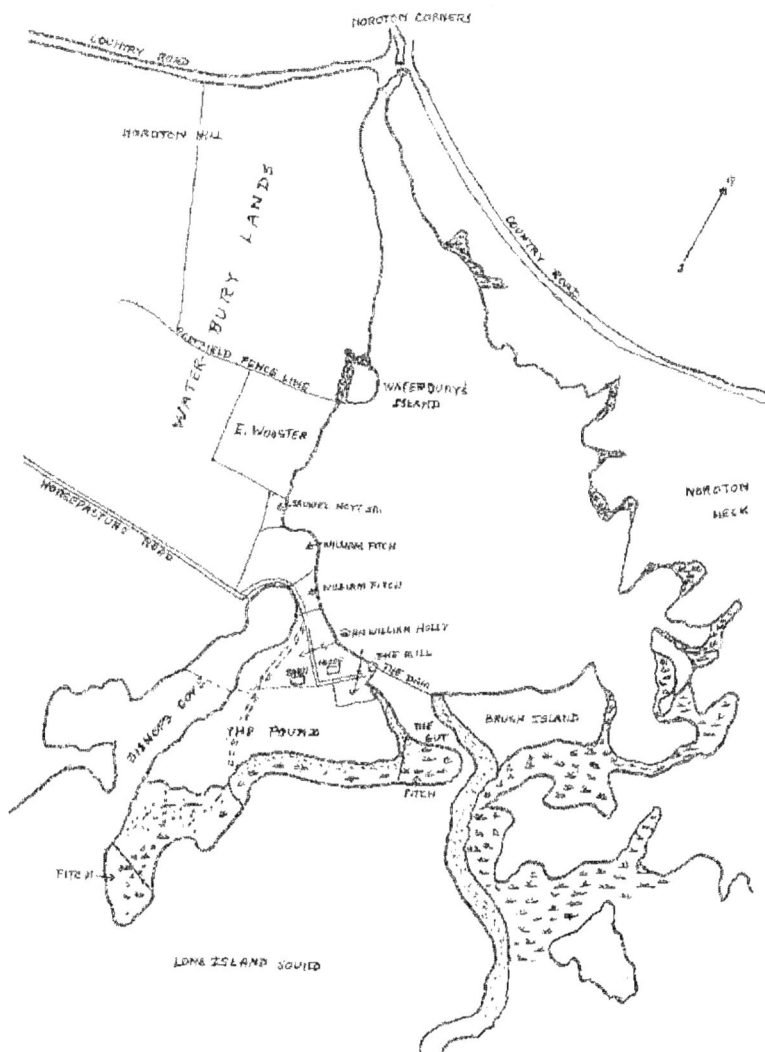

THE COVE AREA IN THE EARLY 1790'S

Sketched by J. Majdalany

other men, Daniel Cotton and James Greenleaf, were also engaged in the enterprise. According to Edward C. Scofield in his "Story of the Cove," they built the mill of "hand-hewn chestnut logs" held together with "hickory pegs or 'tree nails'."[11] The picture of this mill shows it to have been built on the tip of land by the dam. This mill stood until 1894 and in its day was very successful.

What exactly was a gristmill and how did it function?[12] In the first place, it was built, if it were a tidal one, right by the dam so that the buckets of the great water wheel would be filled every time the tide ran out. The wheel would rotate, turning the shaft connected to the top millstone within the building. This stone was so set that it did not actually touch the second stone embedded in the floor. The millstone, five feet or more in diameter and made of local stone in the early days, revolved about 120 turns a minute. The grain (mostly corn and rye as there was little wheat) was fed in a carefully regulated manner from a hopper into a hole through the upper millstone; this was called the eye. Then it was cracked open and crushed by the scorings made in the surfaces of the millstones. These furrows had to be sharpened regularly, and it was no easy task to lift off the top stone (perhaps weighing a ton) to work at its surface with a hammer and pick.

After the grain was ground, cornmeal was run through a sieve, but the resulting rye or wheat mixture had to be passed through a bolter, a cylindrical frame covered with cloth and set on an angle. The chaff would plass directly through as the bolter revolved, and the refined flour would pass through the cloth surrounding the frame. The finer the cloth, the finer the flour so that there could be several grades for the housewife.

A mill could produce about four bushels an hour, but of course a tidal mill was limited by the tide itself. Therefore, eventually, Holly had a number of mill wheels working.

Fitch and Holly were soon buying up the rest of the pound. In 1792 Holly bought an acre from Jonas just below where the mill was built.[13] Then in 1793 Fitch bought five and a quarter acres from Jonas on the mainland just north of his first acre there, though he sold the northern acre and a quarter to Samuel Hoyt 5th.[14] In 1793 also, Phineas Waterbury sold to Holly and the others a half acre abutting the dam on Brush Island.[15] Finally in

12

1795 Holly bought the whole remaining twenty acres of the pound from Jonas, leaving Jonas with only the right to cut sedge in Bishop's Cove.[16] On Holly's first tract of land, four and a half acres, besides the mill were built his own dwelling house and his barn. As has been previously mentioned, he had been living in a house on Elm Street, left him by his grandfather. His daughter Maria Theodosia was born there in 1788 and so was a son who died and was buried in the graveyard on the property. In 1793 John William sold his home there and moved his little family to a lovely new home on the pound. It was situated on a level place within easy reach of the mill to the east, and it afforded beautiful views north over the millpond to the little village of Noroton and south over Long Island Sound. Rebecca, the young wife, must have been happy at her work in such lovely surroundings, though in winter the wind must have made them all button up warmly.

The tax lists of 1793 and 1794 afford us a little view of Holly's assets.[18] In 1793 he had two "smokes" or fireplaces in his home, two cows, a horse, and only fifteen acres in all. He was also taxed for a watch, a luxury in those days. The following year he owned a pair of oxen and had sold all his land but that on the pound. Also, we learn from two land deeds that same year that his barn was to the west of his house across the road that came down from the neck, or William Fitch's land, turned at right angles below the barn, and passed just south of the house to the mill by the water.[19]

John William must have loved his island domain, for he lived there the rest of his life (till 1838). Over the years only two small pieces of land to the east and to the west were specifically set aside as mill property, along with the necessary road, of course. The place became known as Holly's Island or the Island, and John William Holly's residence there consisted of a house and various "outbuildings."

Today when walking across the island, one approaches a large comfortable home, which now contains the offices of the Park Department. This, though, is not an eighteenth-century structure and it is what is known as a "mansion house." However, tucked in on the eastern side of it is a little attached building, now looking very dilapidated with windows boarded up and

13

The dam today. View across to Brush Island.

John William Holly's house, built in 1793, as it is today.

John William Holly's house seen through a mill gear from the East Mill. Courtesy of the Park Dept.

The east side of John William Holly's house as it is today.

shingles loose and hanging. This was John William's early house, though it may well have been moved and changed considerably when his mansion house was built later. Although it does not have a central chimney as many eighteenth-century houses did and although it does have a built-in porch, above which are original dormer windows on the second floor (rather unusual features), it does have a good many eighteenth-century characteristics. For example, the front door is an early one, though glass has been placed in the upper line of panels at a later date, and there are wide pine floor boards with rose-headed nails. At the present time there are five full rooms downstairs and upstairs there are four. If, as is hoped, the house is analyzed extensively and repaired, the total original structure may be determined. For now all that we can say is that there seem to have been about four rooms and two fireplaces on the ground floor. Quite possibly even, at the very beginning, since Holly's family was small and since he was eager to get on with the dam and the mill, there were only the front rooms with an attic above. Fortunately, a great deal of original material still exists so that much can be saved or harmoniously copied.

It is pleasant to think of the Holly family living here as the children were born and grew to adulthood. Maria Theodosia was followed by two brothers, John Melancthon (1793), William Welles (1795), a sister Elizabeth Abigail (1797), and Alfred Apollos (1800). What fun they must have had exploring the island, swimming, and boating! The boys must have been involved at an early age in all the intricacies of the mill works and in public relations with the neighbors from Noroton across the millpond.

Returning now to a consideration of the mill, we note that in 1794 the first proper business arrangements were set up. Holly sold to William Fitch and to James Greenleaf of New York City a quarter right each (£1500) to the road on his land going to the mill and in the mill and other buildings on the tract of an acre and thirty rods.[20] Daniel Cotton, also of New York City, presumably had the fourth quarter as in 1796 he quit-claimed his right to Holly. Cotton referred to the mill buildings lately built by Holly's dwelling house.[21]

A new shareholder entered the scene when Cotton left. This

A damage claim against the mill in 1796.

Courtesy of Miss Elizabeth Sumner

was John Townsend, also of New York. He bought in 1796 a fourth share from Holly for $4,000 and thus had interest in the mills (evidently two buildings beside each other), the land the mills were on, the wharf, the materials of said mills, the mill dam, the small piece on Brush's Island, and the road past Holly's front garden (probably just where it runs today).[22]

Fitch at this time (of New York City since 1793) sold all his lands at the pound, consisting of the two one-acre points and the four and three-quarters acres at the head of Bishop's Cove, to Holly for $200,[23] and he sold his fourth-interest to John Townsend of New York City, thereby allowing him a half-interest in total.[24]

In December of 1796 James Greenleaf, "of Philadelphia, merchant, now Boston," sold his fourth of the business to a group of merchants in Boston.[25] He referred to it as the Columbia Mill, and during this period the millpond too was referred to in other land deeds as the Columbia Millpond. At this time, according to Mr. Greenleaf, the mill was "now occupied by Mr. Wm. Holly" and contained "twelve pair of stones in good repair." He sold his right for $8,000. Four months later in a foreclosure action against Greenleaf two interesting references were made: John William's barn was no longer standing ("where the barn lately stood") and there were now "10 pair of millstones, 8 boulting wheels and boulting cloths."[26] In 1798 a Robert Lennox then sold the fourth interest to John Townsend for $7,300;[27] and so by 1800 John Townsend, merchant of New York City, owned 3/4's of the Columbia Mill complex, and John William Holly owned 1/4.

In the same year, 1796, a very important development occurred. John William Holly bought an acre of land, with a spring on it, on the western edge of Bishop's Cove.[28] That, with the land he got from Fitch a month later, gave him complete control of the upper half of Bishop's Cove. (Later, in 1802, he was to buy twenty-one acres along the lower western side also.[29])

Shortly before 1800 the decision was made by John Townsend and John William Holly to erect a new grist mill by building a dam across Bishop's Cove and by cutting through the land at the head of the Cove to allow a flow of water through from the millpond, thus providing the necessary water power. This action made the pound a proper island, though the dam itself was a link across.

18

Bishop's Cove and to the north, the millpond, showing the Canal or cut separating the Island from the mainland as made by Holly and Townsend c 1800.

The south part of Bishop's Cove today. The millrace in the foreground.

The double house, or boarding house, near the West Mill as seen in 1964. Courtesy of Mrs. Dater

The center of activity clearly shifted to this western area. Soon houses were needed for the workers employed at the mills, and so two were built on the mainland just north of the new mill. One of these was a double house, which was still standing in the early 1960's; Whitman Bailey sketched it in 1948.[30] It had a fascinating chimney construction — an arched passage right through the masonry in the cellar.[31] Holly also owned the small house built by Samuel Hoyt 5th on the land he had bought from William Fitch in 1793. This was situated to the north by the millpond.[32]

To make all legal with Townsend, Holly sold to him in 1800 a 3/4's right to the acre of land on the west, to a 1/2 acre on the east, and to a 1/2 acre at the head of Bishop's Cove, and the "whole of the cove above where the dam is now erected." John Townsend was also given landing rights on the east side of the Cove south of the dam "for the purpose of free navigation in and out of said cove." Included too was a 3/4's right in a blacksmith's shop and in the new road that joined the two mill locations.[33] We gain a further view of what was going on when Townsend took out a mortgage in 1807.[34] He mortgaged all his real estate to John William Holly for $13,616.16, and his right included the three acres occupied by the mills, two grist mills, two dwelling houses, and other shops and stores.

Sometime between 1800 and 1810 a perceptive traveller lingered for some days in the coastal areas of Stamford and enjoyed his experience considerably. Timothy Dwight, president of Yale, wrote about Stamford in his *Travels in New-England and New-York*. He says:

> The third [interesting section of Stamford], named the Cove, is on the western side of Noroton River. On this spot, in very advantageous situations, have been erected two large mills for the manufacturing of flour and a small village, or rather hamlet, for mechanics of various kinds. The view of the harbor in front, the points by which it is limited, the small, but beautiful islands which it contains, the Sound, the Long Island shore, a noble sheet of water in the rear, the pleasant village of Noroton, and the hills and groves in the interior.is rarely equaled by scenery of the same nature, especially when taken from a plain scarcely elevated above the level of the ocean.[35]

21

The double house and later houses by the West Mill as
sketched by Whitman Bailey in 1928. The east end of Cove Road.

It is interesting that he mentions a hamlet there at that time. What other houses besides those already mentioned can be documented as existing then?

All the lands to the west and north were originally Waterbury lands — Jonathan's, Nathaniel's, and John's. In more recent times John Weed had received a part of this (seventeen acres) from his father, Hezekiah Weed, Jr.,[36] and Elizabeth Wooster had received ten and a quarter acres from Jonathan Waterbury, her father[37]; the Woosters also had bought eleven acres of John Weed by 1790.[38] These were solely lands, without buildings.

However, two houses were built along this western shore in the 1790's. Jonathan Waterbury sold his island (today Weed Circle) to Israel Waterbury in 1794.[39] It was an acre of land with Waterbury's salt marsh and a highway "so-called" to the west and the pond on all other sides. Israel built a house there and sold it in 1796 to Deodate Finch, who sold it again in 1797.[40] In the two last deeds a small cove is mentioned to the north.

The second house was also built by Israel Waterbury, who bought a half acre of land from Deodate;[41] originally it too had belonged to Jonathan Waterbury. This piece was northwest of Waterbury's Island and north of what was called Little Cove. A driftway was its northern boundary. This house is still standing on its same half-acre of land. It faces south but no longer looks out over the Little Cove and salt marsh as those have long since been filled in. It was built in 1797. John William Holly bought it in 1798,[42] and when he sold it in 1809 to Smith Weed, it had a cooper's shop with it;[43] Smith Weed is listed as a cooper in all the tax lists of the early 1800's.

The house today is remarkably unchanged. The central chimney joins what was the kitchen and the sitting room, and there is a small entry area by the front door. Off the original kitchen in an added lean-to is a small bedroom — the borning room of the old houses — which the late owner, Mrs. Kathleen Smith, often used in her last years instead of climbing to the bedrooms above.[44] The house is a typical eighteenth-century farmhouse, saltbox in form.

These two houses were, of course, well up along the little road to Noroton, and since Timothy Dwight spoke of a hamlet in the real Cove area, one must presume that there were a number of small buildings clustered about the New or West Mill.

Smith Weed's house, built in 1797, as seen today from the east.

Although the expansion of the mill complex gave rise to a much larger business enterprise, Townsend was clearly in over his head, for in 1807 he took out another mortgage from a Thomas Franklin for $86,734.50,[45] and in 1811 Holly brought suit against him in order to recover his money (given in the previous mortgage). Foreclosure then followed, and Townsend quit-claimed all his rights to Franklin in 1812.[46]

During the short period that Thomas Franklin owned three-quarters of the mill John William found it necessary to make repairs "to save the . . . mills from waste and further injury and decay." The mills were therefore closed between April and September. Franklin claimed that Holly should pay him damages for the loss of business incurred whereas Holly claimed he should be paid for the repairs he had made. The case was heard in New York, and it was determined that Franklin should pay Holly $77.73 and so the matter should be at an end.[47]

By the time the case was settled, Franklin had sold his newly acquired interest to four men; Robbins and Hicks got 5/12's jointly, Wood got 3/12's, and Byrnes got 4/12's of the three undivided fourths. The 5/12's Holly bought for $8,000 in 1813 so that he had 9/16's, a majority control of his mills.[48]

Throughout the mills' history John William Holly was the true miller or man-on-the-spot. (All the other men involved were of New York City, or in one or two cases of Boston.) It would be fun to have a picture of the man. Was he the typical, well-set, rather sturdy figure of the miller? He must have been a man of considerable vitality able to cope with a multitude of perplexing situations, and he certainly was a man with an eye to the future, for not only was he continually expanding the mill business, but also he was building up a farm on the mainland by consolidating his holdings there year by year. In 1800 he owned only thirty-two acres (most of this the island), by 1811 he had 130 acres, and by 1818 he owned 190 acres in tracts both north and south of Cove Road.[49] He built a farmhouse and other necessary buildings on the corner of Cove Road and what was later called Monjo Lane or Island Heights Circle today. These were located on land he bought in 1817, at which time he owned 4 oxen, 15 cows, 2 horses; previously he had been taxed for 20 sheep, but this category seems to disappear from the tax lists about 1815, and chickens, etc. are not considered at any time.

25

In addition to his own interests John William Holly was not unaware of his civic responsibilities and the town concerns. In 1797 he was one of the subscribers for the setting up of the Stamford Mutual Insurance Company for fire protection, and he became one of its five directors, the others being John Davenport, Jr., David Maltbie, Samuel Jarvis, and George Mills.[50] During the 1790's and early 1800's John William, according to the town meeting records, was a surveyor of the highways year after year — probably those in his own section of Stamford only as there were a number of surveyors appointed.[51] In 1803 he was chosen to be a member of the Connecticut Legislature and was responsible for counting the votes.[52] Then in 1807 he was one of the directors of the Connecticut Turnpike Company, which must have been responsible for the tolls and for the improvement of the Country Road, also known as the Turnpike.[53]

In the town meeting records for 1805 an unusual subject was handled. A ruling was drawn up that no oysters were to be raked from the harbors from May 1st to October 1st. However, John William and four others were chosen to grant "liberty to any person to take them in the within time in case of sickness."[54] Evidently oysters were considered most efficacious to the health!

John William Holly was emerging as a man of dependability and as a man of means. His tax assessment rose from $198.30 (excluding the mill) in 1800 to $558.87 in 1819, a very large rise, $51.39, occurring between 1802 and 1803.[55] One wonders if he might at this time have made extensive additions to his house, for it would have been a logical time in that the west mill was now completed, he was a man of forty with five children between the ages of two and fourteen, and John Townsend, owning 3/4's of the mill business, would have taken much of the onus off Holly's shoulders.

In any case by 1812 John William Holly had clearly made the grade. Of the nine grist mills in Stamford he owned one large complex. He also owned two chairs and a coach, on a par with John Davenport, Jr., Esquire, one of the wealthiest citizens of Stamford; there were only seventy carriages in all among the 783 taxpayers. He still owned a gold watch (among about eight in Stamford), and he was taxed too for a clock. Soon he was paying taxes on his 50-ounce plate silver also.[56]

Something rather drastic seems to have occurred in John

26

William Holly's business during the 1820's. In the town meeting records there are tantalizing references to committees being appointed to look into the situation of "John William Holly and Company" and its mills both in 1825 and 1826,[57] but nothing further is recorded on the subject. Holly himself suddenly had a great need of money, and he took out a series of three mortgages. These mortgages are interesting in that they reveal exactly the extent of the land he owned at the Cove. (Holly, as was the case with so many other men of his day, was involved in a number of land deals in other parts of Stamford.) First, he mortgaged the island "where I now live and also 9/16's of Columbia Mills standing on said premises."[58] This consisted of about 40 acres. Then he mortgaged 90 acres south of Cove Road; this included the New Barn Meadow, so-called.[59] Lastly, in 1828, he mortgaged 80 acres north of the Cove Road, bounded on the north by Smith Weed and on the east by the millpond and the road leading to the mill.[60] In all he gained thereby $11,000.

It is hard to tell just what Holly needed the money for at this time. It is possible that since the mills stopped using water power in 1830,[61] he had to make a considerable outlay of funds in order to modernize his equipment. An advertisement in the paper in 1835 serves to support this claim. John William wished to sell "three pair of first-rate burr mill stones, etc. made to order and particularly under his superintendence."[62] He no longer needed them. Some of his millstones, incidentally, can still be seen today. Between his house and the site of the east mill are five millstones lying on the ground. One is of the type that was banded with an outer rim of metal, and one is turned with the cutting edge up so that the lines of ridges can be seen.

Another reason for his needing money suggests itself in an advertisement in *The Sentinel* for November 9, 1835.[63] It runs:

> Wanted immediately two good hands in preparing Dye Woods. Constant employment will be given to such. Apply to John W. Holly. Stamford (Cove)

John William had become interested in shifting the emphasis of his mill production and may well have met the Sanford brothers, who were developing the dye extract business. They were

John William Holly's mansion house, as it appears today.

East view of John William Holly's mansion house.

the sons of Dr. Clark Sanford of Greenwich and Rye. The doctor had found that ground Peruvian Bark was most effective in combatting "winter fever" during the years 1812-1813." When he died about 1820, his sons carried on the mill, promoted "Sanford's Bark" in the neighboring communities, and soon were investigating dye-extract manufacture.[64] If they had encouraged Holly in joining their efforts, he undoubtedly found it necessary to install different equipment from what he had in his grist mills.

Another possibility as to why he needed money is that having recently built a suitable dwelling house, a mansion house, he found his expenses suddenly mounting. This would, of course, be the building that is attached on the western side to the earlier one and now contains the offices of the Park Department. It is quite well preserved, and since it is owned by the city, it can, fortunately, be cared for as it should be so that John William Holly's work can be appreciated by the generations to come.

The house, as it was originally, may well have had no porch across the front, but the large stones approaching it are probably the early ones.[65] The front door and the shutters are obviously not original, and the siding was undoubtedly clapboard, not shingle. Once inside the house, however, one gains a sense of its genuine integrity. There is an aura of comfort and graciousness in the well-proportioned front hall, which opens out into the back hall by means of a wide archway — a very noticeable feature. The back hall leads straight to the rear outside door, which is the original one, probably. The stairs ascend on the right in the back with a landing and a window across the end. The banister and the well-finished ends to the stair-treads, although not elaborate at all, show careful artistry.

The two front rooms, possibly the sitting room and the parlor or the library, are large, comfortable rooms. The sitting room is enhanced by a chair-rail and a gracious Adam-style fireplace. The decoration on it consists of a frieze of stucco — putti are sporting on dolphins, graceful men and women are gathering fruit, and flower garlands join all together.

The other front room has three interesting features: a cast metal fireplace with flanking Ionic columns (its straight lines give a dignity to the whole room), an oval window on the east which looks out upon the front lawn just beyond the little old

View from the north of the back of John William Holly's mansion house.

The rear door of the mansion house. Note the original features.

Metal fireplace in the library or parlor of John William Holly's mansion house.

The Stamford Historical Society

Adamesque fireplace in the drawing room of John William Holly's mansion house

The Stamford Historical Society

William Welles Holly (1794-1876), son of John William Holly and Rebecca Welles Holly.

Courtesy of Mr. George W. M. Clark

house, and a large double archway, now closed in, which once led to the hall of the small house. It would be interesting to see the effect of spaciousness if it were open as it was originally.

There are two rooms behind these front ones, the east one connecting by a door to the hall near the kitchen in the old house. Across the whole width of the back is a porch with several original features.

Upstairs there are three large rooms, one with a fireplace made of 8'' x 8'' bricks, which are early ones, and two small rooms, their size dependent upon the attic stairs and a corridor to one side. The western one has a small angled fireplace and a closet under the attic stairs.

Both the attic and the cellar are spacious, affording much storage room. On the outer wall to the north in the cellar are a large arch and three irregularly spaced niches in the walls. One wonders what these were used for.

All of these rooms added to those of the older establishment gave a total of about 17 rooms, about half of them bedrooms, enough for all the family, the in-laws, the grandchildren, and the servants, plus guests. All of the family must have rejoiced in the new sense of space after the small quarters of the other house. It was a lovely, gracious home with a view over the island to the water beyond south, east, and north.

Behind the house, forgotten and neglected, is an outhouse, a relic of the old days; it is quite amply provided with seats for two adults and two children. Nearby are two other "outbuildings" seemingly modern and used for storage.

In 1835, when John William Holly was 72 or 73, he wrote his will, in which he left his estate to his wife Rebecca and to his four surviving children, little realizing as he did so that he was creating an interminable financial mix-up for them all. His two special requests were: first, for a room to be reserved for his son-in-law William E. McKinney, now a widower, for as long as he remained single and for as long as the house remained in the family (McKinney died shortly thereafter in 1839); second, that the old family burying-ground, which he left to St. John's Church, should be for the use of his "descendants and no others."[66] He would be sad today to find that all the Holly tombs in it have been moved to Woodland Cemetery and his little plot of land is no more.

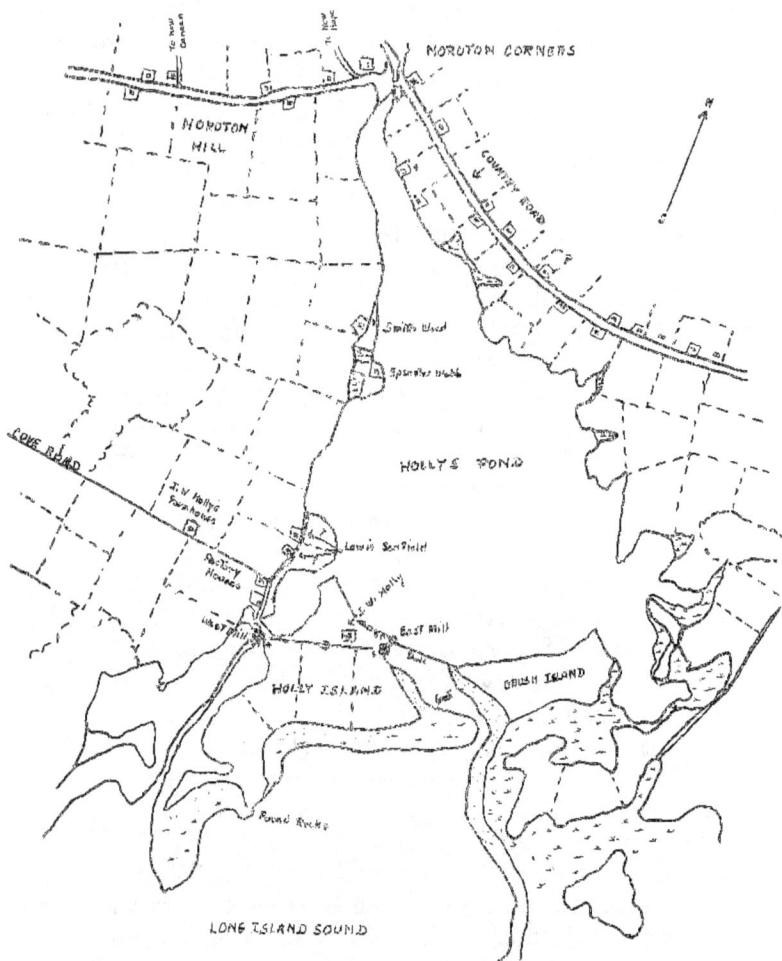

MOROTON CORNERS

COUNTY ROAD

MOROTON HILL

Smith Weed

Spencer Webb

LOVE ROAD

HOLLY'S POND

J. W. Holly's Town house

Lewis Scofield

Factory Houses

E. W. Holly

Webb Mill

East Mill

Mill

HOLLY ISLAND

BRUSH ISLAND

Round Rocks

LONG ISLAND SOUND

TOPOGRAPHIC SURVEY MAP
NO. T-20   1836
with names added

34

During the next year, when the mill was still in John Williams's hands, a map of Stamford was made as part of a United States coast and geodetic survey.[57] It is the earliest detailed map that we have of this region of Stamford, and it is very detailed, marking as well as the types of terrain, the house-plots and the buildings. On it we can find the two wheel-like symbols which mark the two mills, the buildings about the mills, and the eight dwelling houses in the Cove area. It is interesting to note also the very well-settled Noroton Corners.

It is in this same year, 1836, that Henry J. Sanford makes his appearance in the Stamford Land Records.[68] He and his brother, John C. Sanford, were continuing the business of their father in making drugs and were experimenting with dyes also. Their business proved to be successful, and they both were engaged in acquiring mills in several towns. Henry bought the shares that were now owned by Byrnes, Trimble, and Wood. He paid $7,000 and so owned 7/12's of the 3/4's, or 7/16's of Holly's mill.[69] Then in January of 1837 he received a lease from the aging John William, the lease to run for a year with the provision that it could be renewed for three years if such were acceptable to all. Holly leased the mill complex to him for $1,800 a year and made only one provision about the property.[70] The aqueduct was reserved for the use of his house and he was to have access to the pipes on the mill property for repairs, etc. There is nothing new in the list of what the mills and lands covered: two mills, mill dam, outbuildings, storehouses, etc. and the two houses with garden and land just north of the New Mill. Holly still owned all of the island (except for the mill's two or three acres) and his home there; also his farm and orchard to the west and north of the New Mill remained in his hands. The farm work there was largely managed by Charles W. Knapp, who owned half of the livestock and lived in the farmhouse.[71]

On September 23, 1838, John William Holly died, a man who began life as a modest miller and became, largely through his own industry, one of Stamford's wealthy men. He left an estate valued at $32,291.25 in personal effects, real estate, farm stock, and 9/16's of the mill. The farm was worth $10,000, the Island $8,000 and the mills $9,000. The inventory of his personal belongings is given below. These, of course, exclude the rest of the family's, such as his wife's, possessions.

kettle and pans
copper tea kettle
brass clock
bedstead
andirons to stove
7 chairs
bedstead and beds
3 dozen knives and forks
countingroom
sideboard
1 dozen maple chairs
1 sofa
3 maps
carpet
tea set
dining table
8 chairs
1 pair card tables
andirons, etc.
1 lamp
1 cradle
set china, etc.
1 table
5 demijohns
pots, kettles, 6 trays
table and stand
bedstead
washstand
glass and table
carpet
sofa
bedstead
glass and table
carpet and rug
chairs, table and glass
3 dozen bottles
1 brl soap
100 bsh potatoes
bedstead
washstand

milkroom
kitchen stove and furniture
wardrobe
tubs
desk
washstand and table
looking glass
pantry
steelyards
table and stand
8 chairs
1 pair looking glasses
1 spy glass
spoons
plates and candlesticks
oilcloth
tea table
1 carpet 1 stand
5 waiters
1 cot
1 picture
hair carpet
chessboard
bedstead
5 chairs
matting
6 chairs
dressingtable
pictures
books
chess table and maps
6 chairs
2 washstands, etc.
curtains
3 bedsteads
1 brl lamp oil
1 dozen barrels
5 pork barrels
bed
6 chairs, glass and carpet

20 pr linen sheets	10 pr cotton sheets
60 linen towels	30 pr linen pillowcases
12 pr linen tablecloths	12 linen napkins
6 table covers	6 pr blankets
1 tea table	1 night table
1 plate warmer	2 feather beds
china	2 glasses
8 chairs	bed in mill
boots and slippers	coat and pantaloons
drawers	handkerchiefs
5 vests	5 pr stockings
1 coat and pants	2 surtouts
8 cravats	12 shirts
2 hats	shovel, tongs and poker

The list certainly represents a man of means and a man accustomed to many people in his household. There are 68 chairs, for example! One can gain an impression of the size of his household by looking at the census lists for 1820 and 1830.[72] In 1820 there were eleven people living in his home. There were, besides John William and Rebecca, his son Alfred Apollos, who was 20; four men between 26 and 45, two of whom were probably John Melancthon and William Welles, as those two sons are listed two years previously on the tax list: then there were two girls under 16; a young woman under 26, who was probably his daughter Elizabeth (aged 25); and one woman under 45. Again in 1830 there were eleven in the household: John William, Rebecca, Elizabeth and her husband (both of whom were to die in their thirties), four men between 30 and 40, one girl under 15, and two women between 15 and 30. The situation was considerably changed, perhaps only after John William's death, when at some time during the 1830's William Welles brought his family of eleven or so to live there; they are listed in the 1840 census list as living with his mother. It was an ample household at all times.

Unfortunately, John William died with no ready money and with the mortgages still on his estate. His heirs had to pay off $9,588.79 in 1842. Also, the oldest son, John Melancthon, was in financial straits. A week after his father's death he took out a mortgage from his brother William Welles for $7,487 on his share of the estate, and then five years later he was pronounced insolvent.[73] We gain a little more knowledge about the Holly home from an inventory of his belongings there. He had 264 books in the library and elsewhere, bedding, etc., a barometer, a "slay" and a "top carriage," for example. But all of his share in the estate, after his mother's third was subtracted, amounted to only $2,392.32.

After much tedious negotiation between the Sanfords and William Welles Holly, Henry J. Sanford bought the Holly 9/16's of the mill property on June 18, 1842 for $7,250.[74] The deed provides a detailed list of what the mill complex really consisted of — quite different from the little grist mill of the 1790's! The East Mill was still in use with its store houses and wharf; a brand house (where the trademark was applied) was also a part of that complex. The dam and the bit of land on Brush Island were of course included. The shared road south of Holly's house was to be kept in good repair as was the guard wall by the West Mill. The West Mill itself had a store and a brand house, and also a blacksmith's shop on its eastern side. The wharfs and docks and the land along both sides of Bishop's Cove belonged to the mill and so did the Canal Lot where the canal had been cut through from the millpond. Three dwelling houses north of the New Mill went with the property: two were right to the north of the mill itself and one in the middle of three lots to the north of Cove Road along Weed Avenue: Lewis Scofield (noted on the 1850 census list as a miller) was living in it.

Again, the only appurtenance that the Hollys held on to, aside from a right to the road, was the aqueduct which brought water across from a so-called fountain just at the beginning of Cove Road. The water came from their farm to the west and was carried to their house where William Welles was now residing.

On the same day, June 18, 1842, in order to make up the money for the mortgages of John William Holly, his heirs took out a mortgage from Sanford for $2,000 on the Island (their 30 acres with dwelling house and outbuildings).[75] They continued to hold most of the farm land, but a year later William Welles took out a mortgage on his share of it.[76] He moved to Geneva, N.Y., soon afterwards and turned over his share of the farm to his mother.[77]

39

It would be well now before turning to the story of the mill under new management to conclude the story of Holly's Island. It is probable that as Sanford continued to expand the business of the mills, the large comfortable residence situated right between the mills lost its appeal as a seaside home. In any case, after various quit-claims and passing of ownership among the family members, Maria Theodosia Hudson, the oldest child of John William, who was now a woman of sixty-three and lived with her family in Hartford, sold the Island with buildings and 23 acres of land and the aqueduct to the mill company in 1851 for $4,500.[78] Rebecca, "once of Stamford, now of New Haven" where William Welles was by that time living, quit-claimed her rights as did others still holding mortgages.[79] Sanford, the same year, gained John Melancthon's one-fourth right in his father's estate, and then in October he passed on his interest in the Island to the mill company of which he was president.[80]

Thus, although John William Holly's farm continued to be Holly property until the end of the century, the core of his holdings, his residence on Holly Island and his mill complex, passed into the hands of enterprising manufacturers. The mill became increasingly all-important and the residence only a convenience to the mill owners.

CHAPTER THREE

MID-CENTURY EXPANSION OF THE MILLS UNDER THE SANFORDS
1838-1860

It was under the aegis of Henry J. Sanford and his brother John C. Sanford that the Cove Mills entered the era of the industrial revolution. Before the 1840's the business had been more or less a family enterprise, but after this time it became a big business concern, eventually Stamford's leading industry.

In 1837 a meeting was called at Hadden's Hotel in Stamford to set up a joint stock company, and on June 10 the Sanfords received the right to go into business processing "dyewoods, dye stuffs, drugs, spices, plaster, extracts, minerals, clays, and paints" with a capital stock of $50,000.[1] Their aspirations as to the products to be manufactured may seem considerable, but actually the Sanfords were primarily interested in producing dye extracts and in using the by-products for the manufacture of drugs.

Although Cove Mills did not entirely belong to the Sanfords in 1837, it must have been considered that Henry J. Sanford would move to complete ownership soon after his leasing of the property. Another grist mill, that owned by David Holly, John William's brother, was bought by Henry J. Sanford in August, 1837;[2] the deed included the millpond, the wharf, and David's homestead, into which Henry moved. This mill was situated at the Waterside, Stamford's harbor area. John Sanford at this time was handling a mill in New Haven, but he soon was involved in the Stamford mills, Henry selling him the docks at Stamford Harbor in 1841.[3] Henry a short time thereafter gave up his "late residence in Stamford"[4] and lived in New York City for several years.

It was in 1844 that the Stamford Manufacturing Company was born. In December the Sanfords called a meeting of the stockholders to elect five directors and the three officers of president, secretary, and treasurer. The five directors were: Henry Sanford (1000 shares), John Sanford (250 shares), Rollin Sanford (250 shares), Isaac B. Redfield (250 shares), and Nehemiah Brown (250 shares). Henry became president and treasurer, and Rollin was the secretary.[5]

41

HENRY J. SANFORD.

JOHN C. SANFORD.

ROLLIN SANFORD.

Courtesy of Mr. Payson

42

As one can judge by the pictures of the three Sanfords, they were fine enterprising people. Fortunately, in the Minute Books of the Stamford Manufacturing Company brief descriptions of all these gentlemen are given, though not until the late 1870's. According to Rollin, "Mr. Henry J. Sanford was a man of unusual force and energy of character; persevering and industrious, he led a life of spotless integrity and left a record as a merchant for promptness, energy and fair dealing...." John C. Sanford "united to the social qualities which so eminently distinguished his brother, a marked talent for mechanical invention. He contributed largely to the development and improvement of the Stamford Mills; with rare generosity he gave frequent assistance to the projects of others and valuable suggestions which often lead [sic] to useful inventions of which he remained the unrecognized originator."[6] Rollin at the time of his death was given a eulogy from which little of a personal nature can be gained; he was a man of "untiring industry," "rare intelligence," "genial humor" and "rare sympathy."[7] Isaac B. Redfield had charge of some of the mills, particularly one in Port Chester which he brought into the company; he was known for his "careful work." Judge Nehemiah Brown, the Sanfords' brother-in-law, took little part in the work of the mills but aided by means of his "decided opinions" and "excellent judgment."[8] However, he did have a young son, Sanford Brown, who became very much a part of the company and travelled considerably until "his health failed" and he died in 1853 at the age of 28.[9]

Once the company had been set up, Henry turned over all the Cove mill premises to the Stamford Manufacturing Company, though he did except the machinery, etc., used in the manufacture of the extracts from dyewoods and other substances and his right to continue operating the same.[10]

It wasn't long before the East Mill and the West Mill were in full swing. The East Mill was largely devoted to drugs, to Peruvian Bark at first. This substance, found in Columbia and Peru, was in great demand because it yields quinine; it proved valuable in treating malaria, fevers, and stomach disorders; in addition it was helpful as a general tonic. The West Mill, at the end of the Cove where large boats could dock, was used for extracting the haematoxylin from logwood (so-called because

South side of the East Mill, with cupola on the top,
and adjoining storehouse as portrayed by Whitman
Bailey in 1953.

The Stamford Historical Society

Painting "Bass Fishing at the Cove" by Lyell Carr, c. 1890's.
Note the tidal gates in the dam.   Courtesy of Mrs. Dater

View of the storehouse and the East Mill behind it, May 9, 1889.
The Stamford Historical Society

the wood was imported in logs). Schooners came from Central America and the West Indies, bearing the very hard, brown-ish red heartwood, entered the Cove after passing the guiding mark on the little island, "Middle Rock" or "White Rock,"[11] marking the entrance, and unloaded at the wharves. The wood was chipped and processed in great vats until the extract (red,blue,and black) was produced that had proved to be excellent for dyeing wool, silk, cotton, or leather. Most of the finished product was then taken to New York City and re-shipped to its final destination. The company had its office in New York at 159 Maiden Lane throughout most of its history.[12]

Improving the facilities at the Cove, such as enlarging the harbor, building the wharves, increasing the mill complex to handle the various operations, must have been a constant challenge to the new mill owners. In 1846 they were allowed by the Town of Stamford to put in a very important adjunct. Although the mills did have water from the millpond, a good supply of unsalted water was needed. Consequently, permission was sought and the right granted to use the water coming from the Noroton River where it was flowing between Rufus Weed's dam and the main bridge at Noroton. Waterpipes were laid through the lands of Nathaniel C. Bouton above the Country Road and then through a strip of land belonging to Charles W. Knapp, on through Smith Weed's land and Epenetus Webb's on Waterbury's Island. From there the pipes passed through mill land and on to the buildings to the south. The owners of the lands involved did gain an asset in that they were able to use the water for domestic purposes.[13]

By 1847 the business was going well enough for Sanford to release his restriction on the extracting machinery.[14] He also conveyed $41,000 to the company, plus other assets: a schooner called "General LaFayette," the machinery at the Port Chester mill, and the steamboat "Constitution" with its steam boiler. John Sanford gave his rights in the Stamford mills to the company, and Isaac Redfield gave the Port Chester mill. Four thousand shares were given out: Henry held 2000, Rollin 1560, John 240, and Isaac Redfield and Nehemiah Brown 200 each. The capital of the company as a whole was increased from $50,000 to $150,000.[15]

Most proudly in 1848 the company received its official seal, and a beautiful impression was affixed to the Minute Book. On it is a little scene of barrels and chests, and around the edge is inscribed the name of the company. Then, alas, someone discovered that the word Manufacturing was missing its "t"; the seal had to be discarded and a new one made![16]

During the next two years the company did well enough to pay its five stockholders the full amount of their investment, and from then on it was paying a sizeable dividend and its assets increased regularly.

In 1854 a new director, Charles H. Leeds, came into the company upon the death of Sanford Brown,[17] thus marking the advent of this important family into the life of the mills. Then two months later, in March, Henry J. Sanford died. This must have been a shock to everyone, for Sanford was only fifty. Something happened to him in Norwalk, for his will, which he made on March 25, was probated there[18] and he died on the same day according to the *Stamford Advocate* of March 28, which extolled him as a notably public-spirited man. In the court proceedings he is referred to as Henry J. Sanford of New York. His immediate heirs were his two daughters, Ann P., who was twenty-two, and Emily, who was eighteen. These two girls must have had a sad life at this time, for they had had in 1840 two younger sisters and their mother Mary, who was still alive in 1850.[19] Now they were alone save for Rollin, who was chosen to be one of three guardians and executors, and an aunt, Nancy M. Sanford, who lived on Cove Road just beyond the Holly lands from 1849 to 1855, at which time she was referred to as a resident of Rye.[20]

In the 1850 census list Sanford was listed as a merchant worth $75,000,[21] and it is clear from his will that he was a man of considerable means. He made bequests amounting to $56,500, $20,000 of which was to his brother John, and $23,000 of which was donated to charities, such as the Colored House, the House of Friendship, and the New York Association for the Poor. The rest of his estate was left to his two daughters equally.

Just where Sanford was living at this time is unclear. Both in 1840 and in 1850 he is on the Stamford census lists. In 1840 he was living in the house he bought from David Holly. Then he moved to New York until 1845 when he bought a house in Stamford north of the Connecticut Turnpike, or the Country Road.[22] This house he owned until June of 1851.[23] Since he sold that house just after the Stamford Manufacturing Company had received title to "the Island," it is very possible that he used the former home of the Hollys when business required his presence in Stamford. (Henry Hudson, Maria Theodosia's son, was in the Holly house in 1850 according to the census.) However, if his wife had just died, he may well have moved in with his sister on Cove Road.

Henry Sanford, although he was not a native son of Stamford, felt the obligation that most of Stamford's business leaders from the beginning of her history have felt towards fulfilling public service. In spite of the very taxing demands of the mill business in both Stamford and New York he found time to serve in the state legislature during the forties and to be a warden in Stamford for six years. He was also a surveyor of the roads at least once, and in 1850 he was appointed a member of a committee set up to name the streets of Stamford.[24]

Upon Henry's death Rollin became president and guided the company's affairs for five years until 1859 when he resigned and turned in 1060 shares.[25] From then until 1867 he had no active role in the company.

The Stamford Manufacturing Company had continued to grow under Rollin's leadership. The year of Henry's death, 1854, the capital stock rose to $200,000. Its assets were $25,000 in real estate and mills and a like amount in merchandise. A year later the business was valued at $125,000, and a list was given of its assets:

The West Mill	$60,000
The East Mill	8,000
The land	10,000
Dwelling houses and barns, etc.	10,000
Mill dams and water privileges	20,000
Upper mill and dam	2,000
Mill at Waterside	5,000
Mill at Westport	4,500
Mill at Portchester	3,500
Mill at Rye	3,000
Schooner Oscar C. Acken	3,000

plus improved and enlarged machinery[26]

It is unfortunate that the number of houses isn't given, but one is mentioned in the Minute Book because it was acquired that year. Isaac B. Redfield had built it on the north corner of Cove Road and what was later Pond Road and is now called Weed Avenue, and it still exists today. Redfield, when he quit-claimed it to George C. Close, had written into the deed "I having erected said buildings."[27] Redfield evidently resigned at that time as only three directors of the company were appointed for that year: Rollin, John C., and Charles H. Leeds.

One fact that isn't mentioned in the Minute Book for 1855 is that there was a serious fire at the West Mill that year.[28] Perhaps this is hinted at in that there was only a 5% dividend. Unfortunately, too, the newspaper for that date in August is not among those on microfilm in the Ferguson Library. There is only one reference, which occurs in the issue of August 31 under the title "The Workmen at the Cove Mills." It says:

> We are informed that our statement in regard to the workmen at the Cove Mills being thrown out of employment in consequence of the destruction of the works by fire was erroneous. The [mill hands] are all employed in getting the mills into operation again.[29]

Probably as a consequence of this disaster "the Cove Engine Company, No. 1, a fire engine and hose company" was formed by the people residing in the Cove area. There were ten members headed by John W. Leeds, Jr., and they were the proud possessors of this engine:

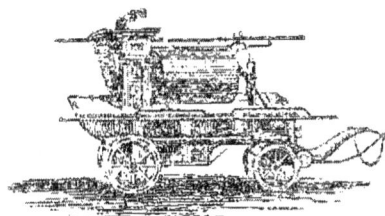

They also adopted the following uniform: "black pants, a red shirt with a star on each side of the collar, a white belt with COVE 1 on it, and a black glazed cap with gilt binding and the letters Cove with a figure 1 on the front."[30]

View of the row of Cove Village houses as sketched by
Whitman Bailey in 1930. Note factory building at
the south end of Pond Road (Weed Avenue).

Naturally, as the Stamford Manufacturing Company expanded its business, much of the Cove area became in one way
or another related to it. Some of the employees needed housing
and were settled into the houses built upon mill land north of
the West Mill. The two houses were occupied by three families
in 1840, according to what one can judge from the census list for
that year. By 1850 one of these houses had been converted into a
boarding house for twenty-three young men under the guiding
power of Coles Weeks and his family.

The logical site for additional housing was on mill property along what is now Weed Avenue. In 1836 there were two houses, as seen on the topographic survey map; then in 1842 the miller Lewis Scofield was living in a house there between a lot and an orchard to the south.[31] He, incidentally, had seven sons ranging in age from nineteen to two. The oldest, Henry E. Scofield, spent his life working for the Stamford Manufacturing Company.

By 1851 there were seven little houses along the west side of Weed Avenue, according to the Woodford Map,[32] and from the census list of the year before, we can tell who was living in them: 1. George C. Close, who was living in Isaac Redfield's house; he was a clerk; 2. John E. Crabb, a carpenter; 3. Benjamin Slater, a laborer; 4. Jonas B. Chamberlain, miller; 5. George Kerrell, a laborer; 6. Cyrus Johnson, a carpenter; and last in the row was 7. Charles Barnes, the superintendent of the dye works.

To the north of the row of factory houses a short distance was the neighborhood schoolhouse, and above that, on Waterbury's Island, Epenetus Webb still lived with his wife and five children. He was a rather poor man, a fisherman, and in 1856 his home came into the hands of William Webb, who owned lands to the west of Smith Weed;[33] Epenetus was still living there in 1870, according to the census list.

Still further to the north James Allen, a day laborer from Ireland, built a small house, which in 1857 he turned over to the Stamford Manufacturing Company,[34] where he worked (most of the mill hands were Irish). He continued to live in the house, though.

Journeying further along the road to Noroton (which road was considerably improved as a thoroughfare in 1856[35]), one would pass Smith Weed's little house, then to the north of it a Federal-style house he had built for himself shortly after 1826. He was still following the trade of cooper, though he was gradually buying tracts of land around him so that in both 1850 and 1870 he was listed as a farmer, but he was on the 1860 census list as a cooper once more.[36] His large house was the last along the mill-pond before one came to Noroton and the Country Road.

As far as the Holly farm lands were concerned, they remained undivided in the hands of John William Holly's heirs. Then in

...ome of Maria Theodosia Hudson and her daughter Maria Louisa, built abo...
...of F. N. Monjo. Home of Mrs. Towne in the background.

Courtesy of...

The Cuthbert Ridley house as sketched by Whitman Bailey in 1951.

View of peninsula on the right where Cuthbert Ridley's house stood.

1854 the Hollys quit-claimed to Maria Theodosia Hudson's daughter, Maria Louisa, a spinster in her late thirties, a tract of land which ran along the top of the ledge behind the Cove houses and over to the Holly farmhouse on the west "now occupied by William Weed."[37] On this land was built an imposing house called "The Cedars." Thus the Holly family still had a base in the Cove area. William Welles Holly and his mother were again living in Stamford by 1857, but William and Ann had bought a house on Atlantic Street away from the Cove.[38] Ann died in 1858 to be followed by Rebecca the following year, and William Welles continued living with his seven children, two servants, and a gardener in his new home.

In 1859 there was a foreclosure case brought against the Holly heirs by James M. Waterbury, who had held a mortgage for some time. He won the case, and then he quit-claimed for a price to each heir his or her portion of the 140 acres west of the Cove.[39] Maria Louisa retained her 30 acres where her new dwelling house was. Maria Theodosia had the farmhouse and the 13¼ acres it stood on to the west of Maria Louisa's land; she also had 25¼ acres south of Cove Road about the oyster pond there. Alfred Apollos received 44¼ acres west of the orchard and south of Cove Road, and William Welles' portion went to a Mr. Candee of New Haven.

One small house was built on what was formerly John William Holly's land. In 1842 Cuthbert Ridley bought from the Hollys three acres on a little peninsula to the southwest of the harbor, and he sold it in 1854 to Charles W. Mead, who lived there for some fifty years.[40] Today there are brick ruins of flooring and chimney base as well as a protecting wall by the water's edge, but whether these are the remains of Ridley's occupancy is a matter for study.

Thus began the break-up of John William Holly's farm, a process that soon accelerated, but for many years not much building went on.

CHAPTER FOUR

TRIUMPH AND DISASTER: 1860 TO 1919

After Rollin Sanford resigned the presidency of the company in 1859 and absented himself from the business until 1867, the management very largely changed hands; only John C. Sanford remained of the old guard. The new directors, Stamford men for the most part, were Charles H. Leeds, who became president, Samuel K. Satterlee, treasurer and secretary, William Gay, and Charles K. June.[1]

At this time the Stamford Manufacturing Company was not only Stamford's leading industry but also it served to place Stamford very notably on the world map. The company was becoming the largest dye extract concern in the world and ready markets existed, particularly in Europe. Although experiments were being made in Germany to develop new dyes from chemicals, there were still many factors impeding that development which was in another fifty years to sound the death knell for the naturally produced dyes. During these fifty years the Cove Mill extracts, the blue, red, and black dyes from heartwood, the yellows and browns from fustic, and the later dyes developed, were much sought after and were highly acclaimed.

The Stamford manufacturers were alert to other possible interests as well. During the 1860's the Stamford Manufacturing Company arranged to process and transport barytes for the Mineral and Manufacturing Company of New Haven. It agreed to "grind, bleach and float" the mineral.[2] Soon the Stamford company was buying and leasing tracts in Cheshire, Connecticut, for mining on its own.[3] Baryte crystals when processed into a powder were used with lead to form a white pigment in paint. The business proved most profitable for ten years, but then the mines gave out. A search for new deposits proved fruitless and even importing barytes from Ireland was not successful.[4]

Another problem at this time was the Civil War. The war years were naturally difficult for any company dependent upon foreign imports and exports as was the Stamford Manufacturing Company. A reflection of this is seen in an entry in the Minute Book for June 18, 1863: "The president is authorized to execute

Tools of the Sheffield Edge Tool Company.

Courtesy of Ronald Majdalany

Courtesy of the Stamford Historical Society

a bond for $2,000 to the Treasurer of the United States for obtaining the drawback in extracts heretofore exported to Europe."[5] The same statement was made the following year. A process of belt-tightening was instituted with good results. Part of the New Haven Long Wharf holdings was sold, as was the mill at Rye.[6] By 1867 the mills were listed as those at Cove, at the Waterside, and at Westport, and the mill business was evaluated at $1,000,000 — a substantial increase from the evaluation of $125,000 in 1855.[7]

Edward F. Leeds became president in 1870 upon the death of his brother Charles, and Rollin evidently returned to be a director when John C. Sanford was unable to continue. John died in March of 1873, and in May of the same year Rollin formally leased the Mansion House with carriage house and garden.[8] His lease included all the northern section of the island above the road that went to the East Mill. He leased the premises for three years at $200 a year. According to the 1860 census list the three Leeds brothers, Charles Henry, John William, Jr., and Edward Francis, were dwelling in the Mansion, and apparently, in 1870 their father, John William Leeds, bank president and a director of the company later, lived there. That same year, Charles Henry and John William, Jr. having recently died, their father moved. In 1878 when he himself died, his residence was on Atlantic Street.[9]

During this period another manufacturing company existed at the Cove. In 1856 James M. Sheffield bought land from Smith Weed and built his house a short distance north of Weed's.[10] Here he set up in a brick building inland from his house the Edge Tool Company. (He is listed as manufacturing cutlery in 1880.) It is believed that he primarily furnished the Stamford Manufacturing Company with such necessities as the metal hoops for their barrels and particular tools that they needed. The Stamford Historical Society has three items made there, a gouge, an adze, and a drawknife, stamped with the name of the company. This factory, however, doesn't seem to have lasted very long, for in 1877 and 1878 James Sheffield mortgaged to William Sheffield of New York a trip hammer and a steam engine with its boiler and pump, and the following year he sold the land.[11]

Below Smith Weed's house along the road to the mills there

was little change in 1870 as to the residents. James Allen's, Epenetus Webb's, and the little row of factory houses, now augmented to nine, remained the sole homes along that part of the millpond. The mill workers living in the row had various positions. In house 9 lived George Washington Toms and his large family. He was a carpenter, and later foreman, in the box factory at the mill, and his great-granddaughter, Mrs. Clara Dippel, now lives in the house. The house today is rather typical of them all, though each is individual to some extent. The gable end faces the street as does a front porch. A small porch at what was the kitchen part of the house is on the south side, and a very irregular brick walk leads from it to the road. The houses are quite small and nestle cozily with their backs to the steep ledge of rock behind. They have over the years had problems with flooding during storms, and large trees help to give an impression of cool and damp. Across the road on the old "Canal Lot" most of the men maintained small gardens.

Mrs. Dippel's house is delightful inside. Originally there were only three rooms on the ground floor — the front sitting room, a small room used for some time as a bedroom, and the kitchen with a pantry and a back shed off it. The house does have a chimney with a front fireplace; Mrs. Dippel says that the kitchen had a stove by the 1840's so that a large kitchen fireplace was no longer needed. Upstairs there were three bedrooms. The ceilings are very low, and a tall man would have to bend his head well on ascending the stairs.

The next house, number 8, was the home of William H. Banks. His son, William C. Banks, became the superintendent of the cooper's shop at the mill. Some of his carving and his mineral collection can be enjoyed at the Stamford Museum and Nature Center. He also had a collection of Indian artifacts from the Cove area which he gave to the New York Museum of the American Indian.[12] Number 7 was occupied by Joseph Paight, Mrs. Dippel's grandfather, for whom the house was built. He was a machinist and later head of the electrical plant. Edward Walker, a watchman at the mills, lived in number 6, and his house might well have been the little grocery referred to by Whitman Bailey in his articles on the Cove,[13] for James Walker, his son presumably, is listed as a grocer both in 1870 and 1880. Ernest Mack lived in number 5; he had eight children at the time. Number 4 was (and is) a double house, which was occupied by George Smith and Charles I. Dayton and their families. The engineer Theodore Scofield lived in the third house for more than thirty years, and the Crabbes, John E. and then his son, George W., who were carpenters, lived from before 1850 to after 1880 in the second house. Lastly, Henry E. Scofield continued to live in Isaac Redfield's and George C. Close's old house; he became the superintendent of the mills about this time.

Of course, below the row were the boarding house, holding as many as twenty people at one time, mostly young unmarried men, and two other houses close to the mill. It is interesting to note how many of the names are Irish. There must have been a warm sense of community among the mill workers.

The severe depression of the early 1870's combined with the failure of the baryte mining served to darken the presidency of Edward F. Leeds. Another problem happened soon after he became president; the company's sturdy schooner of the 1850 days, the "Oscar C. Acken," was sunk by a steamboat called "Elm City" and the company brought suit for damages.[14] The result isn't known, but when the Cove Transport Company began operations in the 1880's, one of its four schooners was the "Oscar C. Acken."[15]

In 1874 the Stamford Manufacturing Company was assessed at $162,107 for its 14 dwelling houses, 30 acres of land, 3 mills, 6 horses, asses or mules, 6 cows, and 2 coaches.[16] The cows are a surprise!

Upon the death of Leeds in 1878 William Gay became president, and from this time on the company became really prosperous with a network of markets both at home and abroad. It concentrated on logwood dyes, some spices (such as ginger), licorice, and flavine (a dye and an antiseptic obtained from the black oak). In 1879 the company was importing licorice root in lots of 500,000 pounds.[17] The licorice was in demand both here and in Europe for medical purposes as a laxative and an expectorant. It also was used in brewing, as a flavoring in tobacco, and, as it is known mostly today, as a confectionery. At the Stamford Historical Society there is a small box marked "Stamford Manufacturing Company" with a dark block of licorice inside. Also, there are some small pieces of the licorice root itself;

STAMFORD
1879

Scale 300 feet to an inch.

it retains its potent smell. According to Mrs. Laurence Payson, children loved to chew on the root pieces. Though it was like chewing on cornstalks, the flavor was truly delicious.[18]

Rollin, who had been receiving a salary equal to the president's ($3,400), died in 1879,[19] and two new Sanfords, E. Harrison and William Henry, held interests, but it was Gay's son-in-law, William W. Skiddy, who rose steadily to a position of leadership from the time he joined the company in 1876.

As the 1880's began, the company became aware of increasing competition both at home and abroad, and meetings were held to find means of improving their industry.[20] It was decided mainly on Skiddy's instigation to update and repair the machinery, to experiment on new ways to process the licorice paste, and to work on gaining strong European markets for their extract of logwood; also it was felt that investigation of the Greek licorice root and the market at Smyrna was advisable. The directors decided to employ a full-time travelling salesman. Tremendous energy and expenditure were put forth during the next ten years to gain maximum efficiency and to obtain rights to licorice fields and factories in Turkey, Syria, Spain, and Batoum, Russia. An amusing note appears — the governor of Antioch was sent a camera and a set of chemicals![21] In addition to the trips to the eastern countries, others were made to Virginia for oak bark and to the West Indies for dyewood. The effort paid off. By 1885 15 million pounds of licorice root were ordered.[22] New cylinders, new boilers, new extractors, macerators, brew cutters, and mullers were installed; more sheds and vats and a coal dock and a hoisting engine were added. Also new waterpipes from Noroton to the mill were put in.[23] Buildings made of brick, with a thought to averting fire, were erected. In fact, there was so much expansion that the nearest dwelling house of the three that then existed just north of the West Mill had to be torn down.[24] Lastly, the Waterside mill was sold as it was considered expendable.[25]

In 1885 a joint stock company known as the Cove Transportation Company was formed to handle the freight that was to be carried by water.[26] Its business was primarily in conjunction with the needs of the Stamford Manufacturing Company and its directors were twenty in number, those men who lived and worked at the Cove, such as Henry E. Scofield, George W.

William Wheelwright Skiddy in 1878.

Crabbe, Charles I. Dayton, Theodore Scofield, and George W. Toms, Sr. They owned four schooners, the "Ida Palmer," the "Robert A. Forsyth," the "Oscar C. Acken," and the "Samuel P. Godwin."

Gay was president until 1882 when he was succeeded by W. T. Minor, a former schoolmaster and later governor of Connecticut,[27] as well as husband of the Leeds' sister Mary. He in turn was succeeded in 1889 by William W. Skiddy.[28] The former two may have had short terms, but certainly they helped to build the company to new heights of achievement. The new president, Skiddy, was a dynamic sort of man, an innovator and a man with an immense range of ideas. He it was who saw the company in its days of greatest power and sadly had to watch it die.

As the company grew, it managed to make a number of enemies among the population at large. For many years people had been in the habit of stopping by the office to ask permission to go onto the southern part of the island for picnics and pleasant outings. All was well until the population increase in Stamford was such that too many people came, and some even passed the mill without asking permission. Naturally vandalism developed (windows in the East Mill were broken, fires broke out, even rocks in the dam were dislodged), and finally in 1884 Skiddy proposed enclosing the mill property entirely, thereby keeping out the general public.[29] In order that those living in the Mansion (but who was living there after Rollin's day is not mentioned in the Minute Books) would not have to go through the mill gates every time they wished to use the road, a new bridge directly across from Cove Road and over the "Canal" was erected. Later on even this had to be guarded. Because the public had had the delightful experience of using the island, there was much bad feeling, though really the Island had not been public land since the 1660's. One man, intercepted by Skiddy as he was on his way to a pleasant outing, answered in pique, "I would like to know who in hell owns this property anyhow!"[30]

Also, the Irish workers probably justifiably felt that they were being underpaid. The subject of increasing their wages was raised in 1881, but nothing more is said on the matter in the Minute Book.[31] One does note a little charity on the part of the company: $100 was sent to aid those made destitute by the

Early 20th century view of Noroton Corners showing the bridge over Noroton River, the Halfway House Restaurant, and Weed Avenue on the left.

The Stamford Historical Society

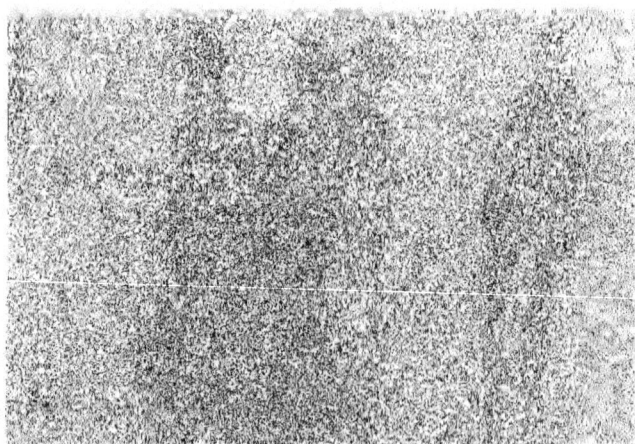

Viola Palmer Pilgrim, Alice Sampon Baker, Clara A. Toms Ryder, Charles G. Toms skating on the millpond.   Courtesy of Mrs. Dippel

flood in Louisville and Cincinnati in 1883, $100 was sent to help erect Bartholdi's Statue of Liberty the same year, and in 1886 $100 was sent to Charleston at the time of an earthquake.[32] Probably since the Stamford Manufacturing Company provided some homes for workers at very low rent (nine dollars a year at one time) and had the mill hands under its thumb, it did care for them in ways not noted in the Minute Books. However, the Irish immigrant workers were undoubtedly exploited as is the case with most immigrants,even today, and there was bad feeling against the mill owners.

Although the general public could no longer enjoy the pleasures of picnicking on the Island, people could enjoy the calm waters of the millpond. Eeling and crabbing were popular pastimes there, no longer enjoyed today. In the wintertime when the weather was severe enough to freeze over the surface, sleigh racing and horse racing were very popular and so was ice skating. In 1893 occurred a memorable 100-mile race in which John Ennis, Joseph Donohue, and Mr. Franklin took part.[33] A much later event that was exciting to Stamford was a fifteen-mile race between Terry Connors (for whom the skating rink at the Cove is named) and Chester Lounsbury.[34] It is too bad that such festivities no longer seem to appeal in Stamford today.

In the 1890's when the picture of Cove Mills was painted (it hangs just inside the front door of the Mansion), the company had reached its peak. It is hard to imagine that the present parking lot and peaceful western end of the Island were once so covered with such a vast array of buildings. The smoke and resulting soot must have been considerable. There were three chimneys, one 126 feet high;[35] there were machine shops, repair shops, vast boiler rooms, storehouses, an ice house, a coal yard with elevators, lines of wharves, a large brick office building, and to tie it all together a narrow-gauge rail track wound throughout for easy transportation.

The licorice business was going well with expanded sources in Batoum, Russia, and John Harris Leeds was appointed to be managing director of the business with the Ottoman Empire and the Empire of Russia.[36] As the company grew, new specialized positions were created. It was at this time, for example, that Willard Parker, Skiddy's son-in-law, was made general manager of the dyewoods and extracts sales departments.[37] In addition to

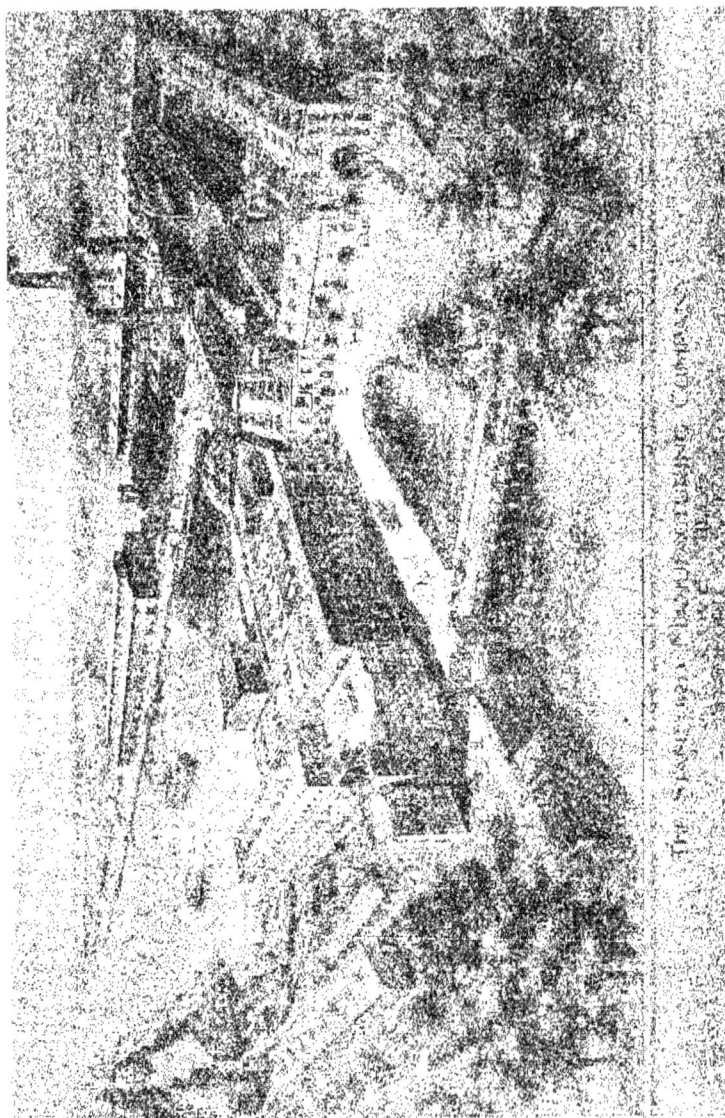

THE SPRINGWELL ISLAND MANUFACTURING COMPANY

Painting made c. 1890. View looking southwest from the island.   Courtesy of Mr. Payson

View of the Stamford Manufacturing Company from the north. From the right — chimney, boiler chimneys, plumbers' shop, tinker shop, machine shop, and on the extreme left the office building.

Courtesy of Mrs. Dippel

The tracks with "car" in front of the office building.
The Stamford Historical Society

h side of the West Mill, showing large chimney and coal elevator.

the new sources for licorice, a new source was found for logwood and fustic in British Honduras and Mexico on the Rio Hondo.[38] Also, the directors bought 29 acres in Lynchburg, Virginia, and built a mill there for the processing of the black oak bark.[39] However, a disaster occurred in the case of the latter, for it burned in 1897 and never did become a success. At the same time the Spanish-American War broke out, impeding commerce in the Caribbean. The Mexican venture proved a problem soon because, although the wood was exceptionally good, it could not be moved out easily; a railroad was needed, an expensive proposition.[40]

At home a minor misfortune occurred, but an unfortunate one for us today. Fire struck the East Mill in 1894, and John William Holly's old mill was deemed not worth re-building.[41]

It is interesting to note that at this time W. W. Skiddy was receiving a salary of $14,000; the other executives, less than half of that, and Mrs. Smith, who was hired as a "typewriter" in 1899, was to receive $20 a week.[42]

From 1900 when the appraisal of the mill's real estate was at its maximum ($693,696.06) and the business was valued at approximately two million dollars[43] to September of 1917, when it was consolidated with a new corporation, which called itself the Stamford Extract Manufacturing Company, the path was all downhill, and downhill for a number of reasons. One reason was that the demand for licorice tapered off, helped by the policies of the Tobacco Trust,[44] and this was a severe loss. In 1902 the company sold its supply of Persian, Russian, Syrian, and Spanish roots and all of its processed green mass, powdered and paste products, its 48 leases, and its factory at Alexandretta in Turkey to a company called MacAnderson and Forbes.[45] It ceased using its trademark Triangle S Brand, and the money received ($460,000) was used for paying its debts and for taking out fire insurance at $200,000; it also bought new fire pipes and a fire pump.[46]

What was not immediately realized, though, was that the equipment at the Cove for processing licorice would thereafter prove useless, and a big loss resulted therefore. Half the mill was closed and a search was made for a new product. The Lynchburg factory was not doing well with selling its yellow dye processed from the black oak because it was running into sharp competi-

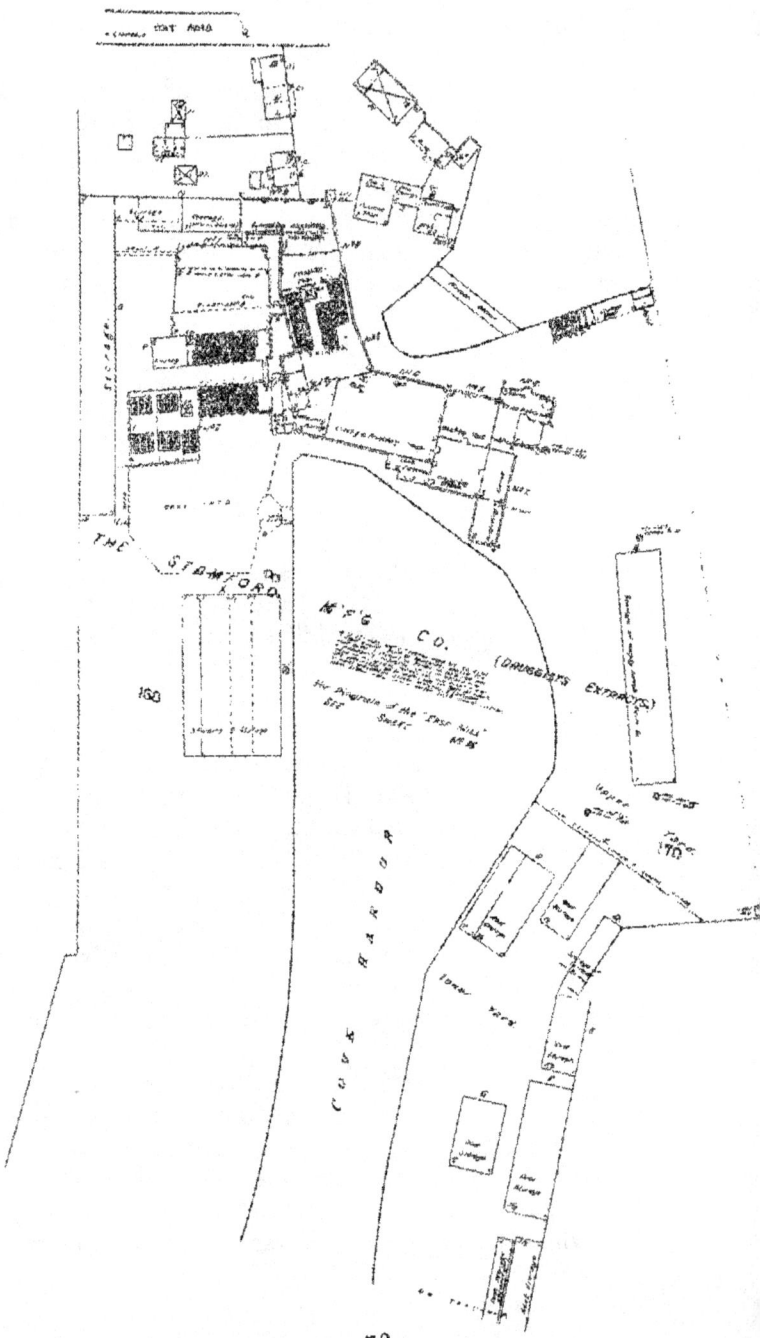

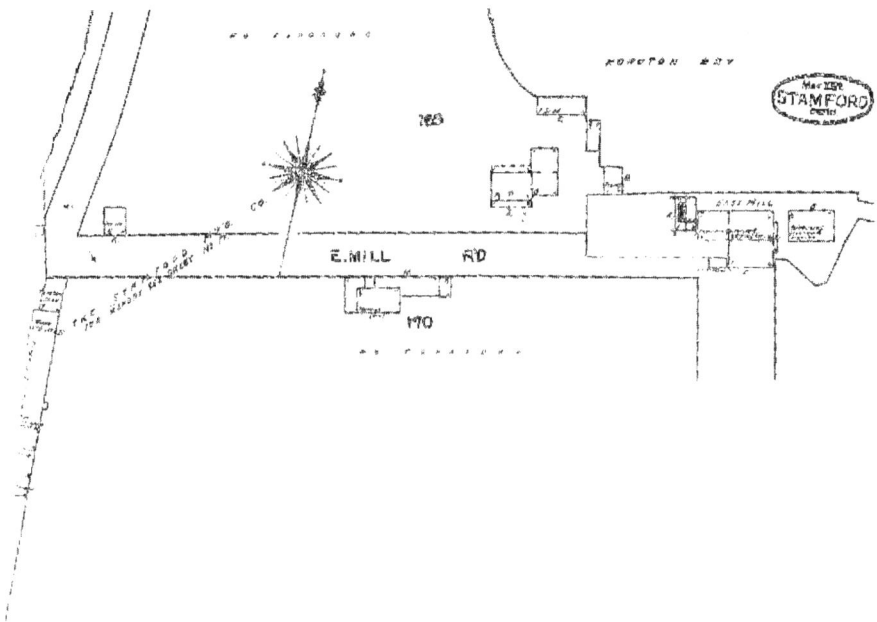

E. MILL RD

MORETON BAY

188

170

tion with the new aniline dyes that were being produced and were eventually to take over the whole market of dyes.[47] That mill was closed but would not even sell until it was dismantled, a further expense.[48] The logwood industry too was naturally affected, and so the Stamford Manufacturing Company turned more and more to using its Mexican land holdings for the cutting of mahogany and cedar and for gathering chickle from the saspodilla tree (used as a base for chewing gum), selling most of the produce to an American company, which did put in a railroad there.[49]

The new product decided upon was a dye from quebracho wood, which is found mainly in Argentina.[50] This red-brown wood contained tannin and could be used in several ways but principally as a dye for leather goods. The Stamford Historical Society has a booklet put out in 1908 by the Stamford Manufacturing Company explaining how the extract was to be handled. In its crude state it produced a strong red, but by refining it and then using it correctly a yellow-to-brown color would be produced. It was an economical and easy process. Some pieces of quebracho wood are also at the Society (as well as a piece of fustic that was stamped with the company's name in the West Indies), and a large trunk of quebracho lies near the millstones east of the Mansion.[51]

At first there was trouble getting the wood out of Argentina because, according to the records, the people of South America were most unreliable.[52] Then new machinery had to be installed, and Cove Harbor had to be enlarged and dredged in order to handle the larger ships needed to carry the wood.[53] The ships came direct to Stamford instead of going to New York where the cargo had to be transferred to barges, as had been done previously. There did seem to be a good market, even in Europe, so that the directors felt much encouraged.[54] Unfortunately, then came the panic of 1907 when demand dropped, and the production had to be shut down for four months.[55] Finally, in 1908 the company was forced to seek a mortgage for $300,000 from John J. Carle, who owned a large drug and extract company in New York and who was Skiddy's close associate. (His son married one of General Skiddy's daughters.) This mortgage was turned over to Skiddy thereafter.[56] By 1912 the value of the mill had dropped to $397,555.34.[57]

Articles of the Stamford Manufacturing Company
now owned by the Stamford Historical Society:

"Branding iron" of the cooper shop with the name
of the company

End of a log of fustic, marked "Stamford Dye-wood
Cove Mills" before it was sent from the West Indies.
This log was removed from Cove harbor.

Ball made of the heavy quebracho wood

Box of licorice stamped with the name of the
company

A piece of a square of licorice paste

Two pieces of licorice root

Courtesy of Ronald Majdalany

A few sidelights on the life going on about the mill can be gleaned from the minute books and serve to add to the total picture of the Cove area during the early 1900's.

In 1901 it was decided that it would be desirable to have Skiddy reside near the mills (as he was living in New York), and so the lower half of Cove Island was leased to him. The lease stated that he would build a residence there and make improvements up to $6,000 worth, and he would pay a dollar a year for rent.[58] He himself designed a rather grand house on the outjutting of rock on the southeast side known as "Pound Rocks" all through its history; this was the name of his home also. Skiddy was a very enterprising man and something of an eccentric too, according to his great-grandson, Mr. William Skiddy Payson.[59] He installed some rather odd features in his self-designed house, such as all-gas central heating, which, however, serviced only the bathrooms. He also installed a strange little passageway for the maid to use "if the doorbell should ring while the family was assembled in the dining room for a meal"; she had to climb up a little ladder in the pantry and pass through an aperture onto a landing on the stairs and go thereby to the front door, all to avoid passing through the dining room! Another hobby he pursued that gives a further view of the man was his making a collection of the exotic insects, beetles, and giant spiders that arrived with the cargoes and displaying them in bottles on shelves in his office. Small boys found these awesome!

Lest one get the wrong impression of General Skiddy, it is important to emphasize how much of himself he put into the Stamford Manufacturing Company. He was constantly aware of deficiencies, ready to meet new challenges, and able to exert true leadership, even though at times quite dictatorially. He also gave of his time and ability to Stamford town affairs, becoming a director in such concerns as a water company and a fire company.[60] Concern for the Democratic party often absorbed him in local political affairs.[61] He also was a world traveller as he pursued his company's interests, and he built up an increasing range of contacts. He even was for a time the treasurer of the Episcopal Church of the United States.[62]

The Pound Rocks house was used by the Skiddys only as a summer home as they continued to live in New York in the

74

House of General William W. Skiddy on Pound Rocks.

Courtesy of Mr. Payson

wintertime. General Skiddy (as he liked to be called because of his political appointment as Commissary General of the Connecticut National Guard[63]) had gardens laid out, some flowers of which still bloom today, interestingly fashioned brick walks set in, and a tennis court made where the Horseshoe Beach pavilion is today. Later, when he decided he was too old for tennis and his daughter needed a home, he built a house for the Paysons on that flat area.[64] When Skiddy died in 1929, his daughter, Mrs. Willard Parker, continued to use his house until her death in 1949.

The Mansion was inhabited by the superintendent of the mills, according to Mr. Payson. However, in the early 1900's Henry E. Scofield was the superintendent and he lived in the first house of the row of nine houses.[65] In 1895 he received a gold watch for his fifty years of service and he died in 1906. He was eulogized as an excellent superintendent, an office he had held for the last thirty years.[66]

Over on the mainland beyond the mill property considerable development was going on towards the end of the century. The last of the Holly land had been sold to developers, and all was broken up into building lots. As more people began coming into the area, the roads had to be improved. In 1878 "the old road from the Cove Mills to the Noroton Bridge" was graded and improved as it was much used and considered unsafe.[67] Then in 1886 the town decided "to widen the road near the former residence of William Weed on the Cove Road."[68] To the latter plan there was remonstrance on the part of Mr. F. N. Monjo, who had bought "The Cedars" and much of the Holly farm and feared that he would no longer have access to the spring beside it. It was pointed out to him that the spring belonged to the Cove Mills as a part of their early deeds from the Hollys,[69] and the work went ahead about 1897. Along this road stores had made their appearance as early as 1878, and one had existed in one of the factory houses, seemingly.[70] The one-room schoolhouse mentioned as being at the end of the factory row of houses had been superseded in 1872 by one built on the northern part of the "Canal Lot";[71] this latter building still exists and is noticeable for its double front door facing the road. This was known as the District 10 school. In 1901 the Stamford Manufacturing Company bought back the land and building, as a new

f the Mansion as it looked in the 1930's and 1940's. Courtesy of

Cove School,[72] named Katherine T. Murphy after the Cove's great teacher, was built further along south of Cove Road towards town.

One strange little area that came into existence about this time was known familiarly as "The Cottages."[73] Fourteen houses were ranged evenly along a little road that led off southwest of the main mill complex. Actually they were shacks of one or two rooms, deemed quite sufficient for the Negro ship loaders and their families who had been brought up from Virginia or the West Indies to handle the really menial work of the company. Although the little settlement did have an air of quaintness and although other families, some Irish ones for example, did move in later, the houses were finally demolished so totally that today there is no trace to be seen.

A rather heartwarming little story is part of the history of the Cove. It concerns a black cabin boy named Theophilus Pompey.[74] He arrived in Bishop's Cove aboard a ship from South America sometime about 1910. Hating his miserable position, he slipped away from his ship and made for the home of one of the Irish families. Unfortunately, he was discovered in the act and two sailors went after him. However, the woman to whose house Theophilus had fled lived up to the spirit of the Irish and kept the sailors off with her broom. Young Theophilus, black though he was, became a true member of that Irish household, calling the family members his father, mother, sisters and brothers. He was brought up as a Catholic and was confirmed by Bishop Nilan in 1912.

In 1914 a dramatic event took place at the Cove, an event of international importance.[75] The English ship "Pass of Balmaha" arrived at the beginning of World War I. After about half a year it changed its registry and became the first foreign ship in Connecticut waters to set forth under the American flag. A ceremony launched it on its way. However, it would have been better had it stayed in the Cove, for it was captured by the Germans, re-named "Seeadler," and as a sea raider allowed its commander, Von Luckner, nicknamed "The Sea Devil," to destroy $25,000,000 of Allied shipping.[76]

To return once more to the story of the Stamford Manufacturing Company, we find that during the early 1900's the rapid increase in the development of aniline dyes was becoming an

Cove Harbor, July 15, 1909

"Duncrag"
    983 tons quebracho
"Brookside"
    915 tons quebracho
Lighters

"Edgar Ross"
    427 tons logwood
"C.D. Pickels"
    552 tons logwood
Freight Prep-"Van Wyke"
Courtesy of Mr. Payson

Three- and four-masted schooners from South America.
Courtesy of Mrs. Dippel

79

Piles of logwood on the east side of the harbor. Warehouses behind. "Cars" on the track.

Courtesy of Mrs. Dippel

Logwood being unloaded from the freighter "Vitalia". Cooper shop on the west side.

Courtesy of Mrs. Dippel

insurmountable challenge to the natural dye business. Germany and England were producing relatively inexpensively a great variety of chemical colors, chiefly from coal tar; also they were overcoming the chief weakness of the colors fading in sunlight. It was impossible for the natural-dye manufacturers to compete with the multiplicity of beautiful aniline-dye colors that were being produced. Then, too, in 1914 war once again seriously interfered with the business of the Stamford Manufacturing Company. From 1914 on, the company struggled, with Skiddy trying desperately to salvage a dying concern.

The workers must have been particularly hard hit. In 1916 it was decided to give a bonus to the employees each January if they passed the following criteria: they had to have been employed for one full year; they had to have done good work; they were never to have had any liquor on the premises; and they must have observed the company rules.[77] A total of 106 men qualified for the bonus, and $3,525 was expended in this way.[78] In a suit that had taken place in 1899 over the matter of building a dam on the Noroton River (which would have cut the flow of water used at the mills), it was stated that the Stamford Manufacturing Company was an important business, employing 300 men.[79] Therefore, from this figure we can estimate that approximately a third of the employees were eligible for the bonus. Probably the purpose was to seem generous and to have the bonus act as a sop to the struggling workers at a time when the mill was in difficulty.

By 1917 a change had to be made. Skiddy formed a corporation with three New York businessmen, holding for himself the position of chairman. The new company was called The Stamford Extract Manufacturing Company.[80] Skiddy himself was to receive a token salary of $5,000 as was James Harvey Scofield, the manager. The deed of sale from the Stamford Manufacturing Company to the new company on January 3, 1918, lists eleven tracts of land: the Island of 47.982 acres, the little piece at the end of the dam on Brush Island, 32 acres on the mainland where the main factory was, 3 acres south of that but separated by the small cove there, the tract with the dwelling houses along the west side of Weed Avenue, four very small tracts along the east side of Weed Avenue, and lastly two small pieces by the dam on the Noroton River.[81]

And so the Stamford Manufacturing Company, proud of its renown throughout much of the world, vigorous, enterprising, and known through the years as most honorable in all its business dealings,[82] passed into history.

The Stamford Extract Manufacturing Company struggled on during 1918, but its report at the end of the year is pathetic. It had transferred its real estate to the Cove Investment and Improvement Company, a holding company, and was leasing the property.[83] No quebracho could be brought in, and only 10,000 tons of logwood had been imported from Jamaica. However, it was thought that "the close of the war [would] make a vast difference" and that with "great care" exercised the following year, the business would pull through.[84]

However, this was destined not to be. On February 19, 1919, the end came through fire, a fire that was devastating indeed. It happened at about 7 p.m. and lit the sky so that people gathered from some distance and many remember the awesome sight. A strong northwest wind was blowing, and all fire equipment proved virtually useless. According to Mr. William White, who witnessed it, the whole widespread scene was truly spectacular with flames and firebrands and exotic colors bursting forth everywhere.[85] The horror was frightening for those in the Mansion. Mrs. Edith Scofield Murray, daughter of James Harvey Scofield, remembers the night all too well. Members of the two families dwelling there climbed out onto the roof to prevent the sparks from catching on.[86] Fortunately, the firemen were able to save both houses, the Holly one and the Skiddys' at Pound Rocks, but the factory itself was a raging inferno in spite of all the prevention installations designed to handle just such an emergency — buildings built of brick, fire walls, special hydrants, and fire equipment.

Mr Payson tells an amusing story about General Skiddy's reaction. It is said that he was attending the opera in New York that evening, and when the superintendent's call came through and he heard the news, all he had to say was, "Do you realize that you are interrupting me in the middle of the second act?"

The article in the *Stamford Advocate* the following day estimated the loss at $2,000,000 and called it the most disastrous fire in Stamford's history. All that was left of the considerable complex the next day was the brick office building

View of the mill buildings after the fire of 1919.

View from the south

View of the jumbo cylinders now lying north of East Beach. Through archway can be seen remains of a cutter.

Courtesy of Mrs. Dippel

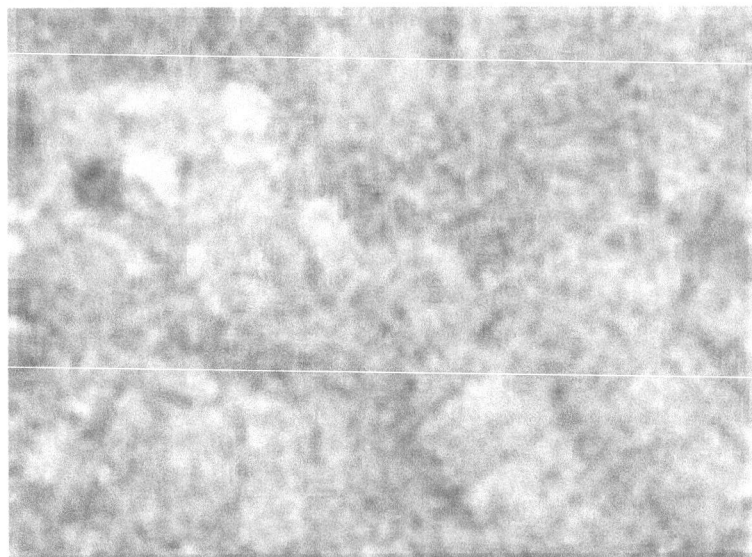

Boilers for steeping the chips of logwood.

Courtesy of Mrs. Dippel

Over-all view of the ruin. Cove area beyond.

Courtesy of Mrs. Dippel

The laboratories and the office building.

Courtesy of Mrs. Dippel

where Skiddy had his office on the second-floor righthand side, a building or two on the island north of the road, and the wharves on the west side of the cove. The smokestacks, the large brick chimney, and remains of the kilns could be seen amongst the rubble.[87] Mrs. Murray says that the fire smoldered for several days.[88]

CHAPTER FIVE

A COMPLETE CHANGE OF SCENE
1919-1978

The destruction of the mills at the Cove was really the final blow, as far as the dye company was concerned. Skiddy, now an elderly man, realized that anyone with the energy to rebuild would have to do so on a vast scale in order to develop an aniline dye business, the only practical course; he saw too what this would ultimately do to the Cove area of Stamford; and he turned against all such prospects. The decision was made not to re-build, not to endeavor to continue the famous dye and drug business.

Naturally, a very sudden change of outlook was faced by the inhabitants of the area. The workers, about 500 men, were without jobs and had to find their way towards making a living. Although they had, on the average, made $1.25 for a ten-hour day and often had to work nights as the mill never closed down, they did have steady, assured jobs at the Stamford Manufacturing Company.[1] Also, those living in company houses awoke to the fact that they didn't even own their homes.[2] There existed bitter resentment against the mill owners and particularly against Skiddy, who continued to enjoy his summer home on the island amid comfortable luxury. Especially during the depression of the 1930's were the workers embittered to the point that they threw stones at the Skiddys when they travelled along Cove Road.

The Lindbergh kidnapping at this time also had its effect on the Skiddy family; their island became a kind of fortress and the Payson children were isolated during their summer vacations, unable to have friends in the neighborhood.[3]

Normally, though, relations were distantly cordial. General Skiddy enjoyed a horseback ride from his home up to Noroton and back and nodded graciously to his neighbors as he passed.[4] The old gentleman was a familiar figure but not well known by the general public.

General Skiddy, maintaining his office at the Cove, supervised the dismantling of what was left of the mills and the clear-

Sketch of the chimney, Cove houses, dock, and office building
by Whitman Bailey in 1931.

Present-day view of the site. First of the Cove houses, that of
Isaac Redfield, center right.

ing away of the debris. Some of his work can be seen today, for he decided to anchor the shifting sands north of the East Beach and to protect the beach by implanting twelve of the steam boilers end to end on the spit of land. They were 60 feet long and weighed 15 tons each.[5] Gradually over the years they have settled and become somewhat covered with sand, but they have served their purpose well. The whole of the island was recognized, of course, as primarily Skiddy land, though he did continue to rent out the two parts of the Mansion. Some business was carried on in the office building as for a while the company used its assets under the names of the Stamford Dyewood Company and the Cove Coal Company.[6] Soon, though, the office building was made over into apartments, and rent from the various living quarters provided some income.

The Hoyts, Ezra and Joseph, the latter the pilot of the "Van Wyck" tugboat, had moved from the Cuthbert Ridley house on its peninsula to the south, and that growing family was well entrenched in the fourteen mill cottages by this time. They enjoyed boating and clamming as well as their being employed still by the Cove Mills.[7]

It was after the death of General Skiddy that matters concerning the millpond came to a head. During the 1930's and 1940's much controversy existed between the two towns of Darien and Stamford because the gates of the dam needed repair and the town governments weren't eager to shoulder the burden.[8] In the old days the gates, made of wood in the carpenter's shop, were changed summer and winter. They were taken on shore near the schoolhouse and allowed to dry out.[9] Thus they lasted and were efficient. Finally Stamford paid $350,000 for four new ones with cast iron hinges (instead of forged as they should have been) and they were set into the dam, only to be broken in that most unexpected of storms, the 1938 hurricane.[10] Incidentally, the Paysons were on the island at the time and their house received a raging torrent of water right through it; all of the low-lying part of the island was deeply flooded. The family took refuge with Mrs. Parker at the Pound Rock house, which withstood the battering as did the Mansion, though its chimneys were seen to rock.[11] Naturally, the damage done to the dam was serious and resulted in considerable change in the character of the millpond, the level was changed, and parts of the pond became

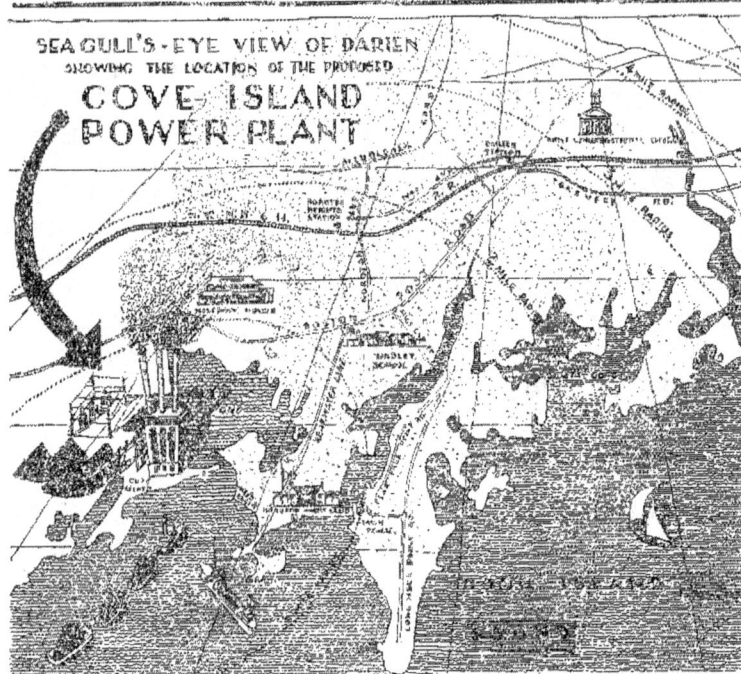

SEA GULL'S-EYE VIEW OF DARIEN
SHOWING THE LOCATION OF THE PROPOSED
COVE ISLAND
POWER PLANT

"WHY A POWER PLANT ON COVE ISLAND WOULD PRESENT 3 SERIOUS THREATS TO DARIEN

1 — SMOKE.... COAL DUST.... WATER POLLUTION!

This plant would be among the biggest ever built in Connecticut! It would pour out 4 tons of ashes every day into the air over Darien. It would have to dispose of 40 tons of solid ashes a day. It would eject sulphur fumes 24 hours a day over Darien. And PREVAILING WINDS BLOW STRAIGHT OVER DARIEN. The plant would be fueled by 10,000 ton colliers polluting the water and bathing facilities with oil, debris and sewage."

The Darien Review, June 19, 1952
Courtesy of Mrs. Dippel

endangered by silting and shifts of current. The two towns continued their running battle.

After many years of trying to sell the Cove property to the city of Stamford, in 1932 the Cove Investment and Improvement Company under the leadership of Robert W. Carle, Skiddy's son-in-law, and Laurence G. Payson, Skiddy's grandson, sold the company's real estate to the Connecticut Light and Power Company.[12] Taxes had been considerable and the land comparatively useless so that the price of $512,000, though low, at least gave the tract a value. Furor then arose over this act, for the inhabitants of Stamford and Darien united at last in protest against having a power station capable of producing 300,000 kilowatts in such a lovely seaside area.[13] Stamford's schoolchildren even got into the act with letters and petitions. The city of Stamford went to court, succeeded in having the land condemned for such an industrial purpose, and finally was able to buy the property for $485,000 in 1955.[14]

During the 1950's, in spite of a certain amount of political graft and again some acrimony with Darien over her dredging work,[15] Cove Island began to take shape as a public resort. It was closed to the public during 1955, and because of general neglect a dump began forming on the mainland at the south end of the former factory complex.[16] Many suggestions were presented as to how the whole area should be treated. A very elaborate plan for an amusement park on the order of Playland at Rye, New York, was fortunately vetoed.[17] Public parking was considered for the area of the Great Meadow in the center of the island, and that too was downed as spoiling the island's beauty.[18] The DAR suggested that the Mansion become a historical museum[19] — an idea that would have saved the house from the deterioration that has ensued. The office building, renovated into seven apartments which were rented, was removed[20] so that only one building, a brick one to the north of the island road, remained of all the mill complex, aside from the little ice house (once stocked by Jeremiah C. Klinefelter of Noroton) now located in the children's amusement park.[21] The main emphasis by the city planners was on keeping the island as a natural park.

Gradually the two beaches were filled in and expanded so that they were a half mile in extent; the East Beach alone could handle a crowd of 256,000 people.[22] A new asphalt road was

View of the 1917 bridge as it is today, looking north to the "Canal Lot" and the millpond.

View of the 1917 bridge, the only remaining factory building, and part of Skiddy's barn as seen today.

The upper millpond, Pond Road (or Weed Avenue), and what was to be called Edson's Park.

The Stamford Historical Society

View of Cove Road with its trolley line in 1931.

The Stamford Historical Society

constructed, and small battery-run trains bought from the 1939 New York World's Fair served to carry people from the parking lot on the mainland to the two beaches. In 1958 a pavilion costing $287,000 was begun at East Beach.[23] A small one had been erected on the former site of Skiddy's tennis court and the Payson house to serve Horseshoe Beach. Fortunately, these were modest structures with bath-house facilities, first-aid stations, and snack bars only; they are low and pleasingly unobtrusive. A fishing jetty was constructed above East Beach so that fisherman could enjoy the sport of catching potential flounder, eels, snappers, smelt, sea bass, and bluefish,[24] but a large pier, which would mar the naturalness of the waterfront, was vetoed. In the 1960's the Skiddy house on Pound Rocks was burned by the fire department as it was found to be a useless edifice,[25] and today people wandering along that lookout point wonder what once was there where bits of wiring, cement, and brick masonry crop out among the rocks. Skiddy's barn, once used for horses and later for early-vintage cars, was located near the south end of East Beach, and it was moved to its present location north of the road and used for storage.[26] Along Cove Harbor itself the rotting wharf pilings remain, serving to demarcate the harbor where to the north is the marina for pleasure craft.

In the Cove neighborhood have grown up over the years countless small homes so that the row of factory houses along the west side of Weed Avenue is no longer isolated; it retains its quaint charm as the homes of the factory mechanics, of the managers of the different concerns of the mills, of the men who handled the company's ships and boats; and those who own the houses today enjoy the traditions they are living amongst. To the north Smith Weed's little house is well tucked in to the west, dwarfed by his larger house and his son Jarvis's stately Victorian mansion to the north. Several other houses of similar nature attest to the prosperity of their owners, who enjoyed the view out over the millpond.

Below them, right by the water is a little park, known as Edson's Park after Gus Edson, the famous cartoonist. It was here that Danny Connors set up his flying school just after World War II with surplus planes he had bought cheaply. No one near the millpond appreciated the heavy planes thundering precariously over their roofs nor did they like the effect on the wildlife

The north side of the Payson house on Cove Island.

Courtesy of Mr. Payson

View of the Horseshoe Beach Pavilion, which incorporated part of the Payson house, 1962.

Courtesy of the Park Dept.

of the pond. And so they banded together to form the East Stamford Taxpayers' Association of 1,435 members. They did succeed in ousting the school.[27]

Waterbury's Island, now Weed Circle, where for a while Mrs. Towne (the daughter-in-law of Henry Towne of the Yale & Towne Manufacturing Company) lived in a house called "The Belvedere," is now a rounded peninsula like the former "Canal Lot" above the Cove, and both are crowded with houses. The former schoolhouse on the "Canal Lot" is now a much modified residence. Everywhere are small, well-tended home lots where once John William Holly's farm and orchard stretched. Even the edge of the millpond has been changed by the building of formal walls (some built by F. N. Monjo[28]) to protect the land from erosion and flood. The millpond, its waters controlled now by immovable gates in the dam (over which the controversy still exists) is a placid body of water attractive for boating, water-skiing, and for swans, ducks, and occasional egrets. However, it is becoming increasingly prone to pollution caused by oil seeping through the drains by the Noroton River. Loyal to their past united efforts, the inhabitants of the Cove area continue to band together to protect their millpond from damage. Recently, they proudly sponsored a clean-up day when truckloads of debris were fished out of the pond and carried off.

It is pleasing to realize, in spite of the inevitable changes, that the Cove retains its basic nature and even its name, though its full name of Bishop's Cove has been lost and, of course, the term is now used to cover a far larger area. At one point it was suggested that the name be changed to honor a Stamford hero, but pressure and a strong letter written by Mr. Russell Roberts of the Stamford Historical Society preserved the time-honored appellation.[29] It is also pleasant to reflect that the island itself, once public land in the 1600's, is again public land and tastefully up-dated for modern use.

Only one important matter demands our attention: Stamford should with all speed call for the preservation and restoration of John William Holly's fascinating double house. There is none like it in all of Stamford, and it remains as the most important building of the old mill days. Will it crumble and be lost, or will it be standing for future Stamford residents to enjoy as a living part of the history of the Cove?

The only remaining part of the factory today.
The Stamford Historical Society

View today looking east along Cove Road to the site of the
Stamford Manufacturing Company.
The Stamford Historical Society

View of Cove Is

Left center: Bishop's Cove and at [...]
West Mill. Center foreground: F[...]
Skiddy house; on the left Horsesh[...]
East Beach. Center middle: Cana[...]
from the mainland and the "Ca[...]
Waterbury's Island, now Weed Cir[...]
ton going north. Right center: "T[...]
dam, and part of Brush Island. Ho[...]
the dam.

Stam[...]

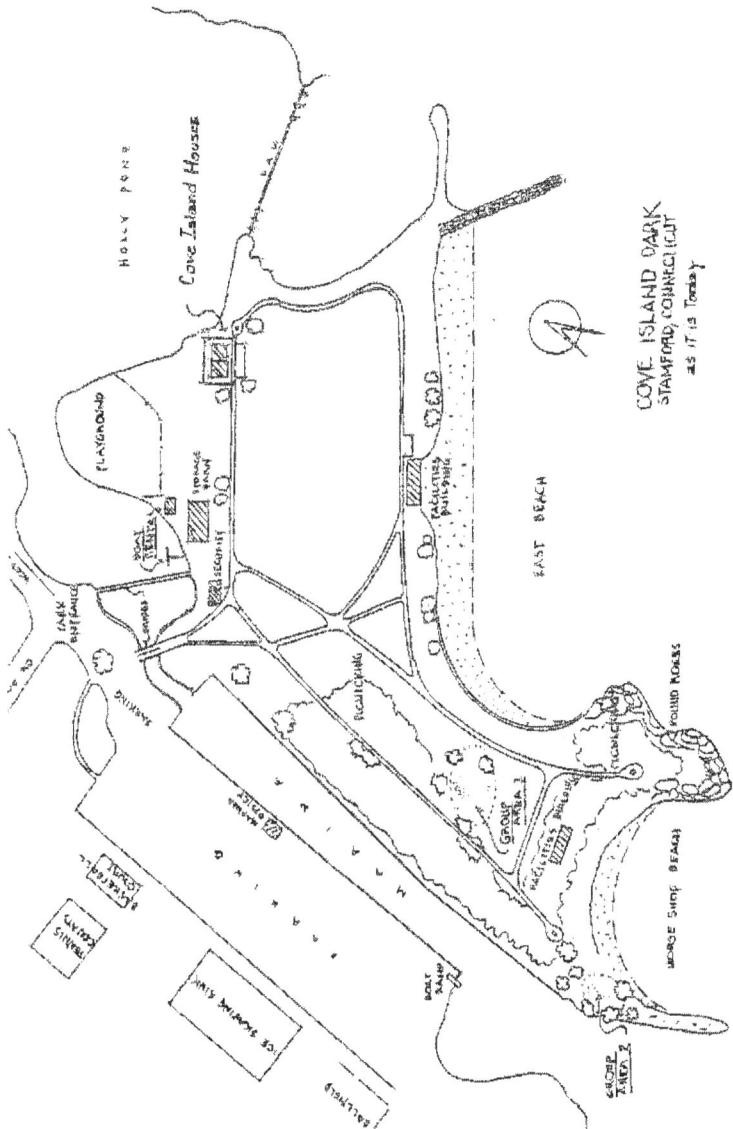

COVE ISLAND PARK
STAMFORD, CONNECTICUT
as it is today

HOLLY POND

Cove Island Houses

PLAYGROUND

STORAGE BARN

SECURITY

POOL FILTER

PARK ENTRANCE

ENTRANCE

PARKING

EAST BEACH

FACILITIES BUILDING

PICNICKING

GROUP AREA 1

FACILITIES BUILDING

PICNIC

ROUND ROCKS

LEDGE SHOP BEACH

GROUP AREA 2

BOAT RAMP

PARKING

MARINA

ICE SKATING RINK

TENNIS COURTS

BASKETBALL COURTS

BALLFIELD

99

View of the northern part of the millpond — Holly Pond today
— looking south.

Courtesy of Mr. Frank Daley

Appendix

The Family of John William Holly

c. 1600-1900

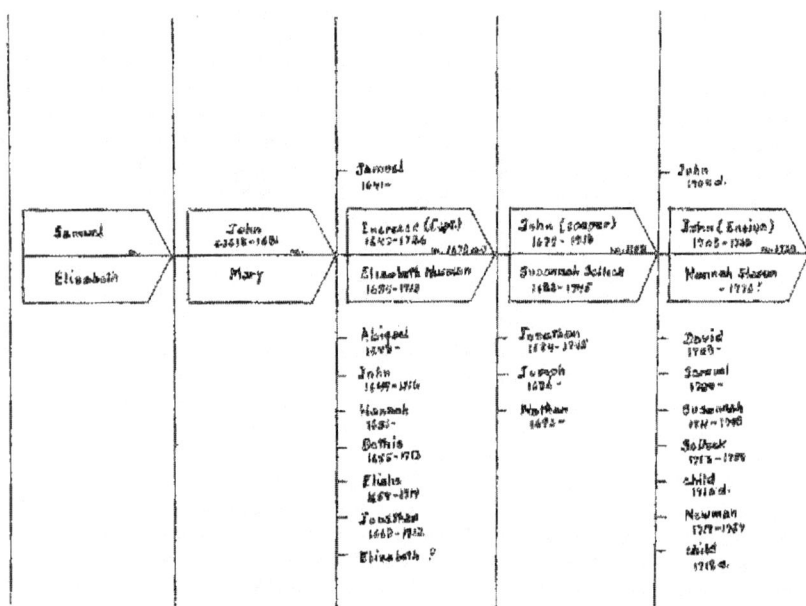

Hannah
1734-1795

Sarah
1780

Elizabeth
1785-1786

John 3rd
1745-1778?

Elizabeth King
1744-1800

Johanna
1738-1840

Hezekiah
1740 d.

John William
1762-1858

Rebecca Walton
1769-1809

Elizabeth
1768-1847

William Ash
1758-1804

David
1769-1802

Martha Coppenholt
1768-1804

Hannah
1771-1820

Thomas R. Smith
c.1748-1847

Mary
1776-1848

Thomas R. Smith
c.1774-1847

Maria Theodosia
1788-1878

Henry Hudson

John Maisonathon
1791-1872

John Melanathon
1793-1872

Clemens Biroh
Clemensia?

William Welton
1794-1896

Ann Glover
-1858

Elizabeth Abigail
1787-1831

Edward A. Mitchwood

William Edward McKenney
1790-1837

Alfred Apollos
1820-1887

Elizabeth Chapman

Mary Catharine Tillman
1817-1866

Mary Turner
1857

John Holly
Melanathon
Maria Louisa
Henry W. (-1805)
Rachelles (1831-1805)
Hannah
William E. Holly
Edward McKenney (-1841)
Elizabeth McKenery

Melanathon IV
Clemenis (Clemandius)
John B

Sarah Rebecca (1839-1873)
John Glover (1838-1858)
Pierre Rousseau (Ross) (1825-1851)
Alice Elizabeth (1870-1945)
Francis Marion (1885-1910)
Henry Hudson (1839-1843)
Edward McKenney (1851-1869)
Mary Welton (1838-1907)

Charlotte Mary Rebecca (1834-1877)
Alfred Tillman (1839-1840)
Charlotte McKenney (1839-)
William White (1841-)
Theron Turner (1835-)

Footnotes

The references to the Stamford Town Records are of three types: the land records, the town meeting records (1866 copy used), and the Probate Court records or file boxes. STR will be used for all of these, followed by the book and page reference for the land deeds; for the town meeting references TM will be used, and for the Probate Court, PC will be used.

Introduction
1. *Stamford Advocate* clippings, 1952-1955, Stamford Historical Society file on the Cove.
2. STR, Book A, p. 194.

Chapter One
1. STR, Book A, p. 265.
2. Estelle F. Feinstein, *Stamford from Puritan to Patriot 1641-1774*, p. 22.
3. The papers of Judge H. Stanley Finch, Stamford Historical Society.
4. STR, TM, p. 277.
5. STR, TM, p. 217.
6. STR, TM, pp. 219 and 221.
7. STR, TM, p. 278.
8. STR, TM, p. 261.
9. STR, TM, pp. 246 and 248. In the *New Haven Colony Laws*, 1656, given in *Records of the Colony or Jurisdiction of New Haven*, p. 605 it states "...It is Ordered, That there shal be one sufficient pound, or more, made, and maintained in every Plantation within this Jurisdiction for the impounding of such Cattel, or Swine, as shal be found in any corne-field, other inclosure, or place prohibited, til it may appear, where the fault, and damage ought to be charged." Courtesy of Mr. Ronald Marcus.
10. STR, TM, p. 261.
11. STR, Book A, p. 101.
12. *Ibid.*
13. STR, Book A, p. 108.
14. STR, Book A, p. 278.
15. STR, Book A, pp. 266 and 338.
16. STR, TM, p. 343.
17. *Ibid.*
18. STR, TM, p. 315.
19. STR, TM, p. 306.
20. STR, Book B, p. 40.
21. STR, Book C, p. 281, 1731.
22. STR, PC, Will of Lieutenant David Waterbury, File Box, 1703. STR, Book B, p. 448, Ebenezer Waterbury to Sarah Weed 1722. ½ Pound from John Waterbury to Jonas or Sarah Weed is not accounted for.

23. STR, PC, Vol. 2, p. 324.
24. STR, Book H, pp. 76, 77, 400.
25. STR, PC, File Box, 1784.
26. STR, Book L, pp. 346 and 515.
27. STR, PC, Vol. 5, p. 346; Vol. 6, p. 464. STR, Book L, p. 271.

Chapter Two
1. Charles Moses Holly, *Record of the Holly Family in America*, 1861, newspaper clipping in the back, Stamford Historical Society.
2. *Ibid.*
3. *Records of the State of Connecticut*, Hartford, 1942, Vol. IV, pp. 310-311.
4. STR, PC, Vol. 7, p. 47.
5. STR, Book K, p. 522.
6. *Records of the State of Connecticut, op. cit.*, Vol. VII, p. 139.
7. STR, Book L, p. 523.
8. STR, TM, pp. 663-664, *cf.* also Book P, p. 286. In *Acts and Laws of His Majesty's English Colony of Connecticut in New-England in America*, printed and published by Timothy Green to the Governour and Company of the above said Colony, 1750, it is stated: "...That no Person within this Colony shall Stop, Damm, or Obstruct any River, Brook, or Stream; or Turn any River, Brook, Stream, or Run of Water out of its Natural Course, with Liberty from the Town in whose Bounds the said Streams, or any of them are." (p. 174). Courtesy of Mr. Russell Roberts.
9. STR, Book L, p. 590.
10. Charles Moses Holly, *op. cit.*, newspaper clipping in the back.
11. Edward C. Scofield, "Story of the Cove," *The Stamford Historian*, Vol. 1, No. 2, p. 147.
12. Catherine Fennelly (ed.), *The Village Mill in Early New England*, pp. 4-10.
13. STR, Book L, p. 641.
14. STR, Book M, p. 177.
15. STR, Book N, p. 352.
16. STR, Book M, p. 139.
17. STR, Book M, p. 117.
18. Tax Lists, Stamford Historical Society.
19. STR, Book M, pp. 175 and 180.
20. *Ibid.* James Greenleaf had been connected with Fitch's mill on Mill River in 1790, STR, Book L, pp. 735, 524, and Book M, p. 32.
21. STR, Book M, p. 258.
22. STR, Book N, p. 235.
23. *Ibid.*
24. STR, Book N, p. 267.
25. STR, Book M, p. 286.
26. STR, Book M, p. 328.
27. STR, Book N, p. 438.
28. STR, Book N, p. 208.

29. STR, Book O, p. 44.
30. Collection of articles and drawings by Whitman Bailey in *The Stamford Advocate* as owned by Mrs. Jean Mulkerin.
31. As recounted by Mrs. Lois Dater, 1978, a personal experience.
32. STR, Book N, p. 238.
33. STR, Book N, p. 605.
34. STR, Book Q, p. 69.
35. Timothy Dwight, *Travels in New-England and New-York*, 1822, Vol. III, p. 352.
36. STR, PC, Vol. 6, p. 464.
37. STR, PC, File box on Jonathan Waterbury, 1787.
38. STR, Book L, p. 420.
39. STR, Book N, p. 328.
40. *Ibid.*, and Book M, p. 309.
41. STR, Book N, p. 322.
42. STR, Book N, p. 448.
43. STR, Book Q, p. 296.
44. Conversation with Mrs. Kathleen Smith, 1975.
45. *Superior Court Records*, p. 161, as referred to in Judge H. Stanley Finch's papers, *op. cit.*
46. *Fairfield County Court Record*, pp. 161-168, as referred to in Judge Finch's papers, *op. cit.*
47. Paper in Holly File, Stamford Historical Society.
48. STR, Book R, pp. 130 and 529.
49. Tax lists, op. cit.
50. Paper in Holly file, Stamford Historical Society.
51. STR, TM, pp. 672, 681, 693, 699, 703, 706, 710.
52. *Records of the State of Connecticut, op. cit.*, Vol. XI, pp. 185-186. Courtesy of Mr. Ronald Marcus.
53. STR, Book Q, p. 8.
54. STR, TM, p. 711.
55. Tax lists, *op. cit.*
56. *Ibid.*
57. STR, TM, Book 3, pp. 91 and 96.
58. STR, Book U, p. 475.
59. STR, Book V, p. 182.
60. *Ibid.* p. 202.
61. *The Stamford Advocate* clippings, Cove File, Stamford Historical Society.
62. Microfilm — *The Stamford Sentinel*, July 13, 1835, Ferguson Library.
63. *Ibid.*, November 9, 1835.
64. Charles W. Baird, *History of Rye 1660-1870*, pp. 169-170.
65. *cf.* Mrs. Virginia Davis (compiler), *Architect's Notes on the Cove Island Mansion and House*, March 30, 1976, Stamford Historical Society, for full details.
66. STR, PC, File box — John William Holly. For further information *cf. Special Acts and Resolutions of the State of Connecticut*, Vol. VII, p.

137 and Vol. XIII, p. 137 and Vol. XIII, p. 125. Courtesy of Mr. Ronald Marcus.

67. U.S. Coast and Geodetic Survey, Department of Commerce, No. T-20.
68. STR, Book Z, p. 645.
69. STR, Book Z, pp. 613-615.
70. STR, Book Y, p. 644.
71. STR, PC, File box — John William Holly.
72. Microfilm — Census lists for Stamford, Ferguson Library.
73. STR, Book Z, p. 703; STR, PC, File box on John M. Holly.
74. STR, Book 26, p. 716.
75. *Ibid.*, p. 719.
76. *Ibid.*, p. 505.
77. *Ibid.*, p. 769.
78. STR, Book 31, p. 184.
79. STR, Book 30, pp. 692-694.
80. *Ibid.*, pp. 695-696; Book 28, p. 460.

Chapter Three

1. *Stamford Manufacturing Company Minutebooks* (to be called *SMCM* hereafter), Book 1, page 1, in the possession of Mr. William Skiddy Payson.
2. STR, Book Z, p. 645, and Book 26, p. 196.
3. STR, Book 26, p. 250.
4. STR, Book 26, p. 277.
5. STR, Book 28, p. 33.
6. *SMCM*, pp. 244-246.
7. *Ibid.*, pp. 239-240.
8. *Ibid.*, p. 246.
9. *Ibid.*
10. STR, Book 28, p. 34.
11. Newspaper clippings, Cove File, Stamford Historical Society.
12. *SMCM*, *passim.*
13. STR, Book 28, p. 716.
14. STR, Book 28, p. 152.
15. *SMCM*, p. 11.
16. *Ibid.*, pp. 17-18.
17. *Ibid.*, p. 31.
18. Norwalk, Connecticut, Probate Court Records, Vol. 12, pp. 78-79.
19. Microfilm — Stamford Census Lists for 1840 and 1850, Ferguson Library.
20. STR, Book 29, p. 570; Book 33, p. 189.
21. Microfilm — Stamford Census List for 1850, Ferguson Library.
22. STR, Book 29, p. 102.
23. STR, Book 31, p. 286.
24. Microfilm — *The Stamford Advocate*, 1843, 1845, 1848, 1850. Also E. B. Huntington, *History of Stamford Connecticut...*, pp. 448-450. STR, TM, Book 3, p. 161, 1840.

25. STR, Book 39, p. 3; *SMCM*, Book 1, p. 49.
26. *SMCM*, Book 1, p. 39.
27. STR, Book 32, p. 383.
28. Huntington, *op. cit.*, p. 452.
29. Microfilm — *The Stamford Advocate*, August 31, 1855, *op. cit.*
30. Cove Fire Department booklet, Cove File, Stamford Historical Society; *Resolves and Private Laws of the State of Connecticut*, Vol. III, p. 513. Courtesy of Mr. Ronald Marcus.
31. STR, Book 26, p. 716.
32. Stamford Historical Society.
33. STR, Book 31, p. 123.
34. STR, Book 35, p. 98.
35. STR, TM, Book 3, p. 271. The road is also referred to in 1809 — *cf.* STR, Book Q, p. 296.
36. Microfilm — Stamford Census Lists 1850 and 1860. *op. cit.*
37. STR, Book 33, p. 163.
38. STR, Book 34, pp. 482 and 568.
39. Judge H. Stanley Finch's papers, *op. cit.*
40. STR, Book 26, p. 715.

Chapter Four
1. *SMCM*, Book 1, p. 50.
2. *Ibid.*, p. 63.
3. C. E. Fritts, *The Barite Mines of Cheshire*, pp. 15-16.
4. *SMCM*, Book 1, p. 180.
5. *Ibid.*, p. 76.
6. *Ibid.*, pp. 73 and 89.
7. *Ibid.*, p. 98.
8. *Ibid.*, p. 132; STR, Book 51, p. 36.
9. STR, PC, File box — John William Leeds.
10. STR, Book 34, p. 759.
11. STR, Book 53, p. 687 and Book 56, pp. 48 and 412.
12. Conversation with Mrs. Clara Dippel, 1978.
13. Whitman Bailey, "Old Banks House," *The Stamford Advocate*, August 18, 1951.
14. *SMCM*, Book 1, p. 113.
15. STR, Book 65, p. 16.
16. Stamford Assessors Book, 1874, p. 161.
17. *SMCM*, Book 1, p. 223.
18. Mrs. Laurence Payson, Conversation on tape, 1966, Stamford Historical Society.
19. *SMCM*, Book 1, pp. 217 and 239.
20. *SMCM*, Book 2, pp. 16 *ff.*
21. *Ibid.*, p. 147.
22. *Ibid.*, p. 105.
23. *Ibid.*, p. 136.
24. *Ibid.*, p. 60.
25. *Ibid.*

26. STR, Book 65, p. 16.
27. *SMCM*, Book 2, pp. 33 and 36.
28. *Ibid.*, p. 132.
29. *Ibid.*, p. 83.
30. Recounted by Mr. William Skiddy Payson, 1978. Also on tape of 1966, Stamford Historical Society.
31. *SMCM*, Book 2, p. 21.
32. *Ibid.*, pp. 62, 69, 125.
33. *Stamford Advocate* clippings, Cove File, Stamford Historical Society.
34. Accounts given by Mr. Frank J. Daley and Mr. Gerald J. Rybnick, 1978.
35. Edward C. Scofield, *op. cit.*, p. 149.
36. *SMCM*, Book 2, p. 280.
37. *Ibid.*
38. *Ibid.*, pp. 204 and 264.
39. *Ibid.*, p. 256.
40. *Ibid.*, p. 287.
41. Edward C. Scofield, *op. cit.*, p. 148.
42. *SMCM*, Book 3, pp. 21 and 24.
43. *Ibid.*, p. 29.
44. *Ibid.*, p. 30.
45. *Ibid.*, p. 75.
46. *Ibid.*, pp. 81-82.
47. *Ibid.*, p. 112.
48. *Ibid.*, p. 157.
49. *Ibid.*, p. 143.
50. *Ibid.*, p. 123.
51. Recounted by Mr. Frank J. Daley and Mr. Gerald J. Rybnick, 1978.
52. *SMCM*, Book 3, p. 123.
53. *Ibid.*, p. 99.
54. *Ibid.*, p. 89.
55. *Ibid.*, p. 186.
56. STR, Book 134, p. 96.
57. *SMCM*, Book 3, pp. 214-216.
58. STR, Book, 134, p. 92; *SMCM*, Book 3, p. 61.
59. Recounted by Mr. W. S. Payson, 1978.
60. *Resolves and Private Laws of the State of Connecticut*, Vol. V, pp. 48 and 264. Courtesy of Mr. Ronald Marcus.
61. Estelle Feinstein, *Stamford in the Gilded Age, passim*.
62. Recounted by Mr. W. S. Payson, 1978.
63. *Ibid.*
64. *Ibid.*
65. Microfilm — Stamford Census Lists 1860 and 1870, *op. cit.*
66. *SMCM*, Book 2, p. 252, and Book 3, p. 152.
67. STR, TM, Book 4, p. 106.
68. *Ibid.*, p. 400.
69. Paper on the widening of Cove Road, Mr. W. S. Payson's papers.

70. Edward C. Scofield, *op. cit.*, p. 150; Whitman Bailey, *The Stamford Advocate*, 1952.
71. Scofield, *ibid.*; *SMCM*, Book 1, p. 121; STR, Book 51, p. 314.
72. *SMCM*, Book 3, p. 43.
73. Recounted by Mr. Thomas Purcell, 1978.
74. Recounted by Mr. William White, 1978.
75. Recounted by Mr. W. S. Payson, 1978. Picture of the ship in his possession.
76. "Luckner," *The Columbia Viking Desk Encyclopedia*, 1953, p. 376.
77. *SMCM*, Book 3, p. 237.
78. *Ibid.*, p. 255.
79. STR, Book 96, p. 149.
80. *SMCM*, Book 4, Sept. 5, 1917. The pages are not numbered in this book.
81. STR, Book 220, p. 10.
82. Edward T. W. Gillespie, *Picturesque Stamford*, p. 238.
83. STR, Book 220, p. 10; *SMCM*, Book 4, May 1918.
84. *SMCM*, Book 4, Dec. 14, 1918.
85. Recounted by Mr. William White, 1978.
86. Recounted by Mrs. Edith Scofield Murray, 1978.
87. Microfilm — *The Daily Advocate*, Feb. 20, 1919, pp. 1-2.
88. Recounted by Mrs. Edith Scofield Murray, 1978.

Chapter Five

1. Recounted by Mr. James Connor and Mr. Edward Monjo, 1978.
2. Recounted by Mrs. Jean Mulkerin, 1978.
3. Recounted by Mr. William Skiddy Payson, 1978.
4. Recounted by Mr. Gerald Rybnick, 1978.
5. *Stamford Advocate* (1925) newspaper clippings, Cove File, Stamford Historical Society.
6. *Stamford Directory 1926*, Stamford Historical Society. Also Mr. Edward Monjo.
7. Recounted by Mr. Gerald Rybnick and Mr. Thomas Purcell, 1978.
8. *Stamford Advocate* (1938) newspaper clippings, Cove File, Stamford Historical Society.
9. Recounted by Mr. Gerald Rybnick and Mrs. Clara Dippel, 1978.
10. Recounted by Mr. Frank Daley, 1978.
11. Mrs. Laurence Payson, conversation on tape 1966, Stamford Historical Society.
12. STR, Book 684, p. 102.
13. *Stamford Advocate* newspaper clippings, Cove File, Stamford Historical Society.
14. STR, Book 771, p. 201.
15. *Stamford Advocate* newspaper clippings, Cove File, Stamford Historical Society; also vertical file on the Cove, Ferguson Library.
16. Vertical file on the Cove, Ferguson Library.
17. *Ibid.*

18. *Ibid.*
19. *Ibid.*
20. *Ibid.*
21. Recounted by Mrs. Clara Dippel, 1978.
22. Vertical file on the Cove, Ferguson Library.
23. *Ibid.*
24. Recounted by Mr. Frank Daley, 1978.
25. Recounted by Mrs. Lois Dater, 1978.
26. Mrs. Laurence Payson, Conversation on tape, 1966, Stamford Historical Society.
27. Recounted by Mr. Frank Daley, 1978.
28. Recounted by Mr. Edward Monjo, 1978.
29. Vertical file on the Cove, Ferguson Library.

Bibliography

"*Acts and Laws of His Majesty's English Colony of Connecticut in New-England in America*, published and printed by Timothy Green to the Governour and Company of the said Colony, 1750.*"

Baird, Charles Moses, *Records of the Holly Family*, 1861 (in the possession of the Stamford Historical Society).

Carter, Robert I., (Virginia Davis, transcriber), *Architect's Notes on the Cove Island Mansion and House*, 1976.

Connecticut Cemeteries Fairfield County Stamford. Connecticut Vital Records Stamford Births, Marriages, Deaths 1641-1852, Barbour Collection, Connecticut State Library, 1925.

The Cove File, Stamford Historical Society.

The Cove, Vertical File, The Ferguson Library, Stamford.

The Darien Town Records: The Land Records.

Dwight, Timothy, *Travels in New-England and New-York*, New Haven: Timothy Dwight, 1822.

Feinstein, Estelle F., *Stamford from Puritan to Patriot 1641-1774*, Stamford, Conn.: Stamford Bicentennial Corp., 1976.

Feinstein, Estelle F., *Stamford in the Gilded Age*, Stamford, Conn.: Stamford Historical Society, 1973.

Fenneley, Catherine (ed.), *The Village Mill in Early New England*, Old Sturbridge Village Booklet Series, Meridan, Conn.: The Meridan Gravure Co., 1964.

Finch, H. Stanley, papers (in the possession of the Stamford Historical Society).

Fritts, C. E., *The Barite Mines of Cheshire*, Cheshire Historical Society, 1962.

Gillespie, Edward T. W., "The Cove," *Picturesque Stamford*, Stamford, Conn.: Gillespie Brothers, 1892.

Hale, Charles R. (comp.), *Headstone Inscriptions*, Town of Stamford, Conn.: Hartford, 1937.

Hoadly, Charles J. (comp.), *Records of the Colony or Jurisdiction of New Haven*, including the New Haven Colony Laws, 1656, Hartford: Case Lockwood, & Co., 1858.

Hoily, Charles Moses, *Records of the Holly Family*, 1861 (in the possession of the Stamford Historical Society).

The Holly File, The Stamford Historical Society.

Hopkins, G. M. (comp.), *Atlas of Stamford and Environs, Connecticut*, Philadelphia: F. Bourquins Steam Lithographic Press, 1879.

Huntington, E. B., *History of Stamford Connecticut from Its Settlement in 1641 to the Present Time. . .*, Stamford, Conn.: William W. Gillespie and Co., 1868.

Mead, Spencer P., *Abstract of Church Records of the Town of Stamford, County of Fairfield and State of Connecticut from the Earliest Records Extant to 1850*, 1924.

Mead, Spencer P., *Abstract of Probate Records for the District of Stamford, County of Fairfield and State of Connecticut* 1729-1802 1802-1853.

The Minute Books of the Stamford Manufacturing Company, Vols. I-IV, in the possession of Mr. William Skiddy Payson.

The Probate Court Records of Norwalk, Conn., Vols. XI and XII.

The Records of the State of Connecticut, Hartford, Conn., Vols. IV, VII, X, XI, 1942.

Resolves and Private Laws of the State of Connecticut, New Haven: Thomas J. Stafford, 1857, Vols. III and V.

Sanborn Map of Stamford, Ct., New York: Sanborn-Perris Map Co., 1892.

Scofield, Edward C., "The Story of the Cove," *The Stamford Historian*, Vol. I, No. 2.

Sherwood, Herbert, *The Story of Stamford*, New York City: States History Company, 1930.

Special Acts and Resolutions of the State of Connecticut, Hartford, Conn., 1901, Vol. XIII.

Special Laws of the State of Connecticut, Hartford, Conn., 1880, Vol. VII.

Stamford Assessors Book, 1874, Stamford Town Hall.

Stamford Directories 1885-1926, Stamford Historical Society.

The Stamford Town Records: the Land Records, the Town Meeting Records, Vols. I-IV, and the Probate Court Records.

The Tax Lists 1782-1819, 1874 (in the possession of the Stamford Historical Society).

Microfilm at the Ferguson Library:

The Greenwich Church Records.

The Census Lists for Stamford 1800-1870.

The Stamford Advocate 1829-1838 and *passim* thereafter.

By correspondence:

Mrs. James D. Murphy ⎫ descendants of
Miss Elizabeth Sumner ⎬ John William Holly
⎭

By interview:

Mr. George W. M. Clark
Mr. James Connor
Mr. Frank J. Daley
Mrs. Lois Dater
Mrs. Virginia Davis
Mrs. Clara Dippel
Mr. Ronald Marcus
Mr. Edward Monjo
Mrs. Jean Mulkerin
Mrs. Edith Scofield Murray
Mr. William Skiddy Payson
Mr. Thomas J. Purcell
Mr. Gerald J. Rybnick
Mrs. Kathleen Smith
Mr. William White

By tapes owned by the Stamford Historical Society:

Mrs. Laurence Payson, 1966, with members of the Stamford Historical Society.

Mr. William Skiddy Payson, 1966, lecture to the Stamford Historical Society.

(sign needed by correspondence.)

Addenda:

The following relevant material has been discovered since this book was written:

One pane of glass from the Holly mansion with initials of some of the Holly children scratched into it; it belongs to the Stamford Historical Society.

A log book of the tug "Runabout" kept from June 1916 to February 1919. The entry for February 20th states, "Mill burned." It belongs to the Stamford Historical Society.

Pictures that belong to Mrs. Jean Mulkerin, one of which gives a partial view of the row of very small cottages built for the workmen and others showing the burning of Mr. Skiddy's boathouse when it was deemed useless.

Copies of five letters which were sent by Miss Elizabeth Sumner. One is written by Rebecca Holly to her mother-in-law about 1797; it gives glimpses of her home life at the Cove. Two were written by Rebecca in 1843, one to William Welles Holly, and one to her family describing her difficult journey from New York to the Cove. One was written by William Welles Holly to John C. Sanford in New Haven, and the final one was the last letter written to the family by John Glover Holly before he was lost at sea in 1844.

INDEX

List of Patrons

Union Trust Company

Hartford National Bank & Trust Company

Constitution Federal Savings & Loan Association

F. D. Rich Company

THE EARLY HISTORY
OF
LONG RIDGE VILLAGE
1700 - 1800

by

Jeanne Majdalany

The Stamford Historical Society, Inc.
Stamford, Connecticut
1977

Cover picture: Long Ridge Village, looking
north along the Bedford Road

Acknowledgments

To several people I wish to acknowledge my indebtedness:

Mrs. Lois Dater I thank for the picture of Old Long Ridge that she found in the files of the Stamford Historical Society and for her general encouragement.

Mrs. Virginia Davis initiated my interest in the Old Long Ridge area during the Bicentennial project of researching the eighteenth-century houses of Stamford; she also offered several valuable suggestions upon reading this history.

The staff members at the Stamford Town Clerk's Office and at the Ferguson Library were always available for help.

The New York Historical Society gave permission to use the portion of the Erskine Map, which is in their possession.

Most of all, I would like to thank Mr. Robert Halliday of the Stamford Historical Society without whose patient help and invaluable aid this study would never have been printed.

Jacob White's house, built about 1749

Preface

This history of Long Ridge Village between 1700
and 1800 is based almost entirely on two kinds of
source material: the recorded land deeds, which are
so fortunately available at the Stamford Town Hall,
and the genealogical material that can be collated
from sources at both the Town Hall and the Ferguson
Library. As a consequence the history tends to be
dry. There is nothing available that I know of that
would give a richer view into the lives of the early
farmers of Long Ridge - no letters, diaries, or on-
the-spot accounts. The earliest source material of
this sort is Frederick Ayres' journal, which he wrote
during the middle 1800's.

As far as the genealogical material is concerned,
I have not given footnotes but have instead included
charts of the two principal families, the Whites and
the Warings, which are the result of the information
accrued from all sources. The bibliography does cover
all genealogical source material.

An explanation is needed about the boundaries
set up for Long Ridge Village. One could make a geo-
graphical entity of Stanwich in that Long Ridge was a
part of that whole district, which covered the Mianus
River area and part of Greenwich as well. However,
for the purpose of having a really limited area with
which one could deal in an essay of this sort, I have
narrowed the bounds to the actual village itself,

leaving out the people, such as David and Frederick
Hait, who lived along the old road to Stanwich, or
Erskine Road; they would have considered themselves
as part of the village though they were outside the
real center.

As to the spelling of the names, I have used
the modern, generally accepted forms. Waring, for
example, appears as Waraing, Warring, and Woren, also later as Warren. I have used the name Waring
throughout.

Lastly, I make no claim for complete historical
accuracy. Undoubtedly others working on this material will turn up facts or realize relationships of
which I am as now unaware. I offer only an effort
to get the available knowledge on paper, to clear up
some inconsistencies or errors that have existed
heretofore, and to present a clear, logical history
of the development of Long Ridge Village.

The Early History of Long Ridge Village
1700 - 1800

A large tract of land in southwest Connecticut
was bought from the Indians in 1640 by Captain Nathaniel Turner. He, representing the New Haven Col-
only, met with two Indian sagamores, Wascussue, who
owned considerable land along the water, and Ponus,
who with his son Onax ruled Toquams or the northern
part of the land. Turner completed a handsome deal
for New Haven; he bought the tract of roughly 128
square miles[1] consisting of "meadows, upland, grass
with rivers and trees" for "12 coats, 12 hoes, 12
hatchets, 12 glasses, 12 knives, 2 kettles, and 4
fathoms of white wampum."[2]

Soon a small group of discontented men in Wethersfield approached New Haven with an offer to buy
the new tract. They wished to leave their town for
the usual reason in New England: religious dissen-
sion, probably mixed with a desire to find better
land for themselves. They bought the new territory
of Rippowam, as it was called, for 100 bushels of
corn, and in 1641 the small band of adventurer-set-
tlers consisting of 21 men left Wethersfield and set
about making new homes where the center of Stamford
is today. The harbor was serviceable, and the river
had good power for the necessary saw and grist mills.

The vast lands about this little settlement were
for a long time not needed, and as the Indians were

1

still about and unpredictable (especially as they
were bewildered by the sudden change in their lives),
the inhabitants of Stamford contented themselves with
consolidating their little village and expanding its
dimensions only gradually.

In 1655 questions arose as to the actual boundary lines of Stamford, and a new treaty was drawn up
for Ponus and Onax to sign. This document stated
that at a point 16 miles north of the town's center,
presumably where the meeting house stood, a boundary
line running four miles to the east and four miles
to the west was to be the northern limit (commonly
referred to as the eight-mile line). Above it was a
two-mile area set aside for the colony's cattle. In
return the Indians, having given up their rights,
were given 4 coats. During the latter part of the
1600's the boundary line between New York and Connecticut was a rather indeterminate one, people buying
or selling land along it or across it without any restriction. The final boundary was eventually set at
what it is today - 10 miles to the north, Stamford
thereby becoming by 1750 a settlement only three-
fifths of its original size.[3] The new line was now
called the eight-mile line, with a four-mile tract
above it that eventually became Pound Ridge.[4]

Long Ridge Village first comes into the light of
history in 1700 when on November 25 the town of Stamford laid out to Major Jonathan Selleck and his brother John 246 acres, which were bounded on the north
by "ye devideing line betweene Connecticut and New

2

Yorke, East by ye hill to ye east of meadows of Stony
Brook, west by Mianus River, south by marked trees
and stone brook [sic] and common land, the rode to be
allowed as it is to pass throw ye sd. land...."[5] The
road referred to, probably once an Indian tract, connected Stamford with Bedford, and it was usually referred to, therefore, as the Bedford Road. It is interesting to note that the main river of Long Ridge,
Stony Brook, had already been named by this time; the
name, however, was by no means an unusual or exclus-
ive one.

Major Jonathan Selleck, once an officer in King
Philip's War, and his younger brother, Captain John,
were prominent citizens of Stamford. They had come
from Boston, had married sisters, Abigail and Sarah
Law, respectively, and had proceeded to build careers
for themselves that resulted in their being the
wealthiest landowners in Stamford. Captain John,
however, did not enjoy his new land acquisition in
the north as he was captured by the French on the
seas in 1689 and never returned.[6] In 1709/10 the
town gave the tract of land in two land deeds to
John Holly, cooper, and Jonathan Bates together;
they were Captain John's sons-in-law. First a tract
of 60 acres was given and then an additional 63. The
boundaries now described show an increase in population in the area. To the north was the eight-mile
line, to the west was the Mianus River and Benjamin
Green's land, to the south was common land, Ferrises
Ridge, and Thomas Newman's land; Jonathan Selleck's
half was to the east.[7]

3

Jonathan's half of the 246 acres became Nathan
Selleck's after his grandfather's death in 1712/13.
Jacob Moon, "chirurgion", (believed to be the first
doctor in Stamford[8]) disputed the ownership for a
time, however. He claimed an interest through his
marriage to Nathan's sister but finally was made to
renounce his "pretence ... to a instrument" he said
he had received from "ye deceased Major Jonathan
Selleck".[9]

Interestingly enough, the tract of land, the
246 acres, remained intact; it turned out to be considerably larger, however, as the subsequent land
grants prove. The parcel was a nice piece of land,
part of it high along the center ridge with views
off towards Long Island Sound, much of it rolling
hillside with ample water, either in brook or pond,
some of it swamp and "boggy meadows", as the section
near Stony Brook to the east of the ridge where the
Bedford Road ran was called. Stony Brook could be
utilized to keep the necessary mills turning, farms
could be productive (as is seen even today), and a
community along the road would be easily in touch
with both Bedford and Stamford.

Just how the three men living on the island of
Nassau (Long Island) happened to hear of these 246
acres is unknown and why they wished to uproot their
families to break new ground is equally a mystery,
but they bought the land in 1717, and they began the
little community of Long Ridge. On July 1 Nathan
Selleck sold his half to Thomas Brush, Jr., James

4

White, and Micaell Waren (Michael Waring), and so did
John Holly, cooper, each for £ 100. [10]   The Bates
family had quit-claimed their interest to the Hollys
in 1710, and Sarah, Captain John Selleck's granddaugh-
ter, whose rights were recognized in 1712/13, must have
agreed to the sale. [11]   In case there remained any
question, all those concerned quit-claimed again in 17-
18/19 and 1722. [12]   The land in this sale was limited on
the east by "ye hills or mountains" (that word seems
rather unjustified!), and the sale included "all tim-
ber trees, wood or underwood, springs, brooks, water-
courses."

Brush and White must have left their families behind in Huntington and Waring, his in Queens Village,
crossed Long Island Sound, trekked inland the ten
miles or so, and set about clearing land and choosing
sites for their homesteads. That these three "tenants-
in-common" were business-like is shown by their having
already decided how to apportion the lands and having
built their houses by November of the following year.
One could say that this was the real date, 1718, for
the settling of Long Ridge Village. These family men
then gathered their household possessions (mainly
tools, bedding, and cooking utensils), their wives and
children, and said their goodbyes to their friends and
relatives. Did they bring along livestock or start
afresh after moving?

James White at this time was in his mid-thirties,
and he already had six children: Stephen, twins
James and John, Israel, and Peter, and a daughter Deborah. His wife Sarah must have found the move all

5

too strenuous, for she died the following year. In
January of 1720/21 James made a formal agreement with
John "Woren" of Oyster Bay in which he promised that
in marrying Elizabeth, John's daughter, he would give
their offspring the right to half his lands in Stamford and elsewhere.[13] James was clearly surmounting
many difficulties in his life at this time.

Michael Waring was forty-one and married to Rebecca Scudder. They had a small son named Jonathan,
only two years old. Jonathan was to live to be the
great arbiter of Long Ridge, the father and grandfather of many, and the grand old man of the village,
dying at the age of 88. Long Ridge definitely agreed with him! Michael's other sons were born during
those two very strenuous years - Scudder in 1718 and
Michael in 1719.

Thomas Brush, Jr. was married to Susana Ketchum
in 1710, and in 1717 they had three children: Eli-
phalet, Phillip, and Elizabeth. However, it is extremely doubtful that Thomas Brush, Jr. ever occupied
his new house, for in May of 1719 he and his wife
sold their share of the tract to John Ingersol, a
husbandman of Oyster Bay. At the same time Nathaniel
Potter, a saddler, and his wife Martha of Huntington
sold the same lands and the house they had bought of
Brush to John Ingersol also; evidently the first sale
hadn't been entirely completed.[14] The Ingersols
thereafter became important members of the Long Ridge
Village and later of Stamford, for Simon Ingersol,
the inventor, was a descendant.

6

The method that the three men, Waring, Brush, and White, used to divide up their 246 acres was one which found its roots in the Middle Ages: the strip system. The value of it was that each landowner was treated as fairly as possible - no one owner would get all the swamp or the good parts of the river for building mills, the best woodland, or meadows for animal grazing. The weakness of this method was that men were handicapped by having non-adjacent pieces of their farmlands so that here in America changes in land ownership, when based on the strip system, came about very rapidly. This was certainly true of Long Ridge. The practice, though, of dividing the land amongst one's sons counteracted any tendency towards land monopolies. A map of White's, Waring's and Brush's land holdings, as recorded on November 13, 1718, has been included herein.[15] By referring to it, one can see that on the east side of the road from the Colony Line south, the strips run White, Brush, Waring, White, Brush, Waring, White, Brush. On the west side they run White, Brush, Waring, Waring, White, Brush. The boggy meadows to the east, about 64 acres, were left undivided. How they made the divisions and allotted them would be interesting to know. The arrangement does create tremendous difficulty for the researcher because two pieces owned by one man can have the exact same boundaries. A tract being sold that is referred to as bounded north by White, south by Waring, east by the meadows, and west by Bedford Road could be in either of two locations and cannot easily be identified.

7

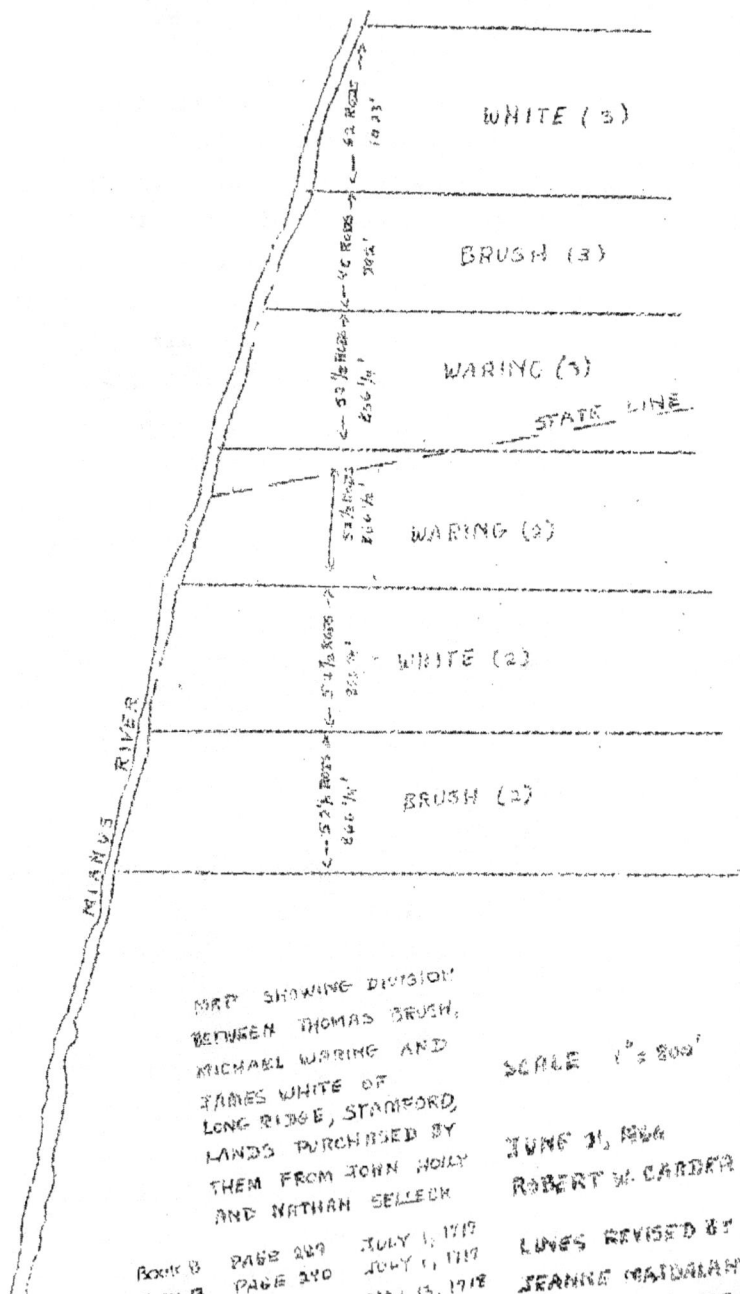

MIANUS RIVER

WHITE (3)

← 42 RODS →
693.35'

BRUSH (3)
← 46 RODS →
759'

WARING (3)
← 53 3/4 RODS →
886 1/4'

STATE LINE

WARING (2)
← 53 3/4 RODS →
886 1/4'

WHITE (2)
← 52 1/2 RODS →
866 1/4'

BRUSH (2)
← 52 1/2 RODS →
866 1/4'

MAP SHOWING DIVISION
BETWEEN THOMAS BRUSH,
MICHAEL WARING AND
JAMES WHITE OF
LONG RIDGE, STAMFORD,
LANDS PURCHASED BY
THEM FROM JOHN HOLLY
AND NATHAN SELLECK

SCALE 1" = 800'

JUNE 21, 1966
ROBERT W. CARDER

LINES REVISED BY
JEANNE MAJDALANY
FEBRUARY 13, 1977

Book B   PAGE 289   JULY 1, 1717
Book B   PAGE 290   JULY 1, 1717
Book B   PAGE 319   NOV 13, 1718
Book B   PAGE 319   NOV 13, 1718
Book B   PAGE 320   NOV 13, 1718

8

COLONY LINE

WHITE (5)

BRUSH (5)

WARING (4)

WHITE (4)

BRUSH (4)

TODAY

DIDISHEIM

LEVINE

KARLSEN

MILLER

JONES

CHILLINGTON

HEALEY EST

GOODWIN

WARING (1)

ST FRANCIS CH.

LOEHN

RECTORY

HILL

CHASE

CONE CH.

WESTON TOLEND

PARSONAGE

BEARD

WHITE (1)

MEADOWS

SILVER BURN 25CH

SOLL'N DIVIDED LAND 32½R 500CH 32½R

HARTMAN

HISHER

NOWLAND

BRUSH (1)

FREY

TARDY

HENNESSEY

SONDHEIM

LOEHN

BINGHAM

DOELING

SPONY BROOK

32½ Rods 266 ¾'

SHERWOOD

ANABLE

BARBER

KRAUS

9

In this division of the lands reference is made to James White's and Thomas Brush's houses. They lived in their southernmost strips on the east side of Bedford Road, and their common line was equidistant from their houses. Another reference was made to James's house when Bedford Road was being formally laid out by the town of Stamford in 1722.[16] His house is marked as 275 rods south of the Colony Line, and it was 208 rods north of where the Branch river crossed the road. If one works this out from the river end, one locates the house as about opposite Parsonage Road, and the Colony Line at that time as about 265 rods north of where it is today. Thomas's house must have been a short distance below James's. Michael's house was also on the east side of the road, in his southernmost strip, probably just north of Rockrimmon Road today; his homestead was later divided between his sons Jonathan and Michael.[17]

In Stamford, the farmhouses of this period, of which there are very few, one being the Historical Society's house of the 1690's, and another the house at 984 Stillwater Road, built in the early 1700's, were simple in basic structure, though some variations did exist. The chimney was the central feature, sometimes as large as 12 to 14 feet square. The front door usually faced south for the warmth and opened upon a small vestibule from which the steep staircase went up, parallel to the front wall; it usually was enclosed to keep the warmth of the house from ascending in the wintertime. On one side of the central chimney was the sitting room, and on the other side was the kitchen. A door led to the cellar, which was used for storage. The kitchen fireplace was spacious to allow for free movement during cooking, and a Dutch oven was let into the back wall so that baking could be done. It was bricked, in dome fashion. Sometimes there were two main rooms and the kitchen was at the back in an added or integral "lean-to"; usually then there were three fireplaces. Upstairs was normally all one room and here the children slept. The great advantage was that innumerable children could be taken care of. Rooms could be fashioned of this upper-room space if it were desired.

Once, therefore, the chimney with its ponderous stones was set and the foundation walls built, the rest of the house could be done readily, provided a saw mill were handy. No doubt the three Long Ridge men gathered their necessary supplies from a mill and set to work together to build their homes.

By 1720 there were four families living at Long Ridge: James White, who had the six children already mentioned and with his new wife was to have seven more,[18] Michael Waring, who had the three boys and later completed his family with two girls; John Ingersol, who had six sons, Nathaniel, Simon, Samuel, John, Daniel, Josiah, and probably two daughters, one married to John Wright. He was given a home by his father-in-law in the northernmost eastern lot.[19]

These four families found it difficult to go
all the way to the Stamford meeting house on Sundays.
Even today to travel ten miles or so to go to church
would seem rather too much, but in the 1720's much
more was expected of the churchgoer. The road from
Long Ridge went steeply downhill to where Hunting
Ridge meets it; then the traveller went steeply up
that, travelled along the crest until descending to
the valley just before Webb Hill; then it was another
climb and another ride along the crest until one descended into Roxbury. The old road, now Stillwater
Road, took one to the "Country Road", then the main
road to Greenwich. The trip by horse must have
taken a good two to three hours, depending on the
weather as well as on the condition of the roads. At
any rate, at the town meeting in 1720/21 the four inhabitants of Long Ridge were permitted to go to
church in Bedford (one half the distance to Stamford)
and to pay the minister's tax there; this was granted
each year through 1724.[20]   At that time presumably a
meeting house was built at Larance's Farm near the
Mianus River for the "convenience of coming to meeting on Sabath days" as had been provided for at the
town meeting the year before.[21]

The other major need was a school. Probably the
children of Long Ridge were at first taught in someone's home and given only a simple education. Possibly, too, the Long Ridge inhabitants used Bedford.
Soon, though, Stamford schools became accessible. In
1721 a school was planned for the Roxbury area, and

12

another was provided in 1727 for the people near Larance's Farm, which before long became known as the
community of Stanwich.[22]   There were close ties between Stanwich on the Mianus River and Long Ridge,
which became included as a part of Stanwich.

Not very much can be learned about the four families during the 1720's, although "Jeams Whit" stands
out in the town meeting records as being appointed a
surveyor of the road for four years.[23]   A surveyor
was expected to check on the condition of the roads
of his designated area, to supervise the group of men
under him in their work on the roads (all men were
expected to do their share of repair work during the
year), and to advise the selectmen when new roads
were needed or old ones were outdated; sometimes he
would have to report when people were encroaching upon the roads with their buildings or walls. James
White undoubtedly was responsible for overseeing the
area above Webbs Hill and over as far as Stanwich on
the river.

In 1726 a sad event occurred. Michael Waring
died during the winter month of February. He left his
wife Rebecca to cope with five children, all 10 and
under. After three years she was fortunate in finding
a new husband, Jonas Weed (the fourth in the direct
line of descent by that name. The first was one of
the earliest settlers of Stamford.) Both Scudder and
young Michael accepted the Jonas Weeds' guardianship,
but nothing at all is said of Jonathan.[24]   No doubt
at the age of eighteen in 1734 he was able to be inde-
pendent.

13

Michael's estate consisted of a house and barn and house lot, which Jonathan later stated was 16 acres;[25] he had a 7-acre tract (the northernmost eastern piece), and his share of the undivided lands. To the west of the road he had 50 acres, according to the inventory, but it seems to have been double that, judging from later transactions.[26] This was quite enough farm land for one man to handle. Constructing the necessary buildings, clearing the land for plowing or for pasturing the animals, and erecting the sturdy stone walls still visible throughout the settlement must have taken its toll of these men.

Three years later James White followed his friend Michael, his son James, one of the twins, dying two weeks before him. He, too, left a young wife, who had to manage with her six children alone. Timothy was only 8, Sarah 6, Jacob 4; then came Richard, who died early, and Uriah, followed by James, who was born that year and named after his deceased half-brother. The five children of the first wife were at least of an age to be of help to Elizabeth. Stephen, the oldest, was married this same year and took on the guardianship of his younger brother Israel.[27] Stephen also gained a position of prestige in Stamford by taking over his father's job of surveyor of the roads.[28]

During the 1720's changes in land ownership took place; as several deeds are unrecorded, it is difficult to understand the total scene. However, as these families mainly preferred to build their homes

14

close to each other in Long Ridge, it is possible
to determine fairly closely where each one lived.

When the Ingersol children came of age in the
1730's and were given lands as they married, several
houses were built. Aside from the one above the 8-
mile line which John Ingersol gave to his son-in-law
John Wright, who sold it in 1729[29], he had two other
houses, one in his southeastern piece, which presum-
able had been Thomas Brush's, and one on his middle
piece east of the road. The latter he gave to Simon
(John signed his deeds with his "mark" only): Simon
sold it to his brother-in-law John Jaggers.[30] Nathaniel, another son, received the southern half of
the tract along the road to Stanwich, and he built
his house inland on it.[31] The Brush house on its
17 acres was sold to Isaac Quintard in 1727, but John
Ingersol seemed to live there all the same, and in
1737/38 it was returned to Nathaniel, who sold the
south half to Simon, mentioning his father to the
north.[32] Simon built a new house and barn for himself on that 8-acre tract.[33] The third son, Samuel,
probably received the Brush house upon the death of
his father, but there is no record of it. He was
later to build a new house on his same piece of property. The ease with which the Ingersols put up
houses suggests that they were the ones who began the
saw mill on Stony Brook, particularly as later they
took on an interest in another mill near Greenwich.

15

Long Ridge in the 1730's

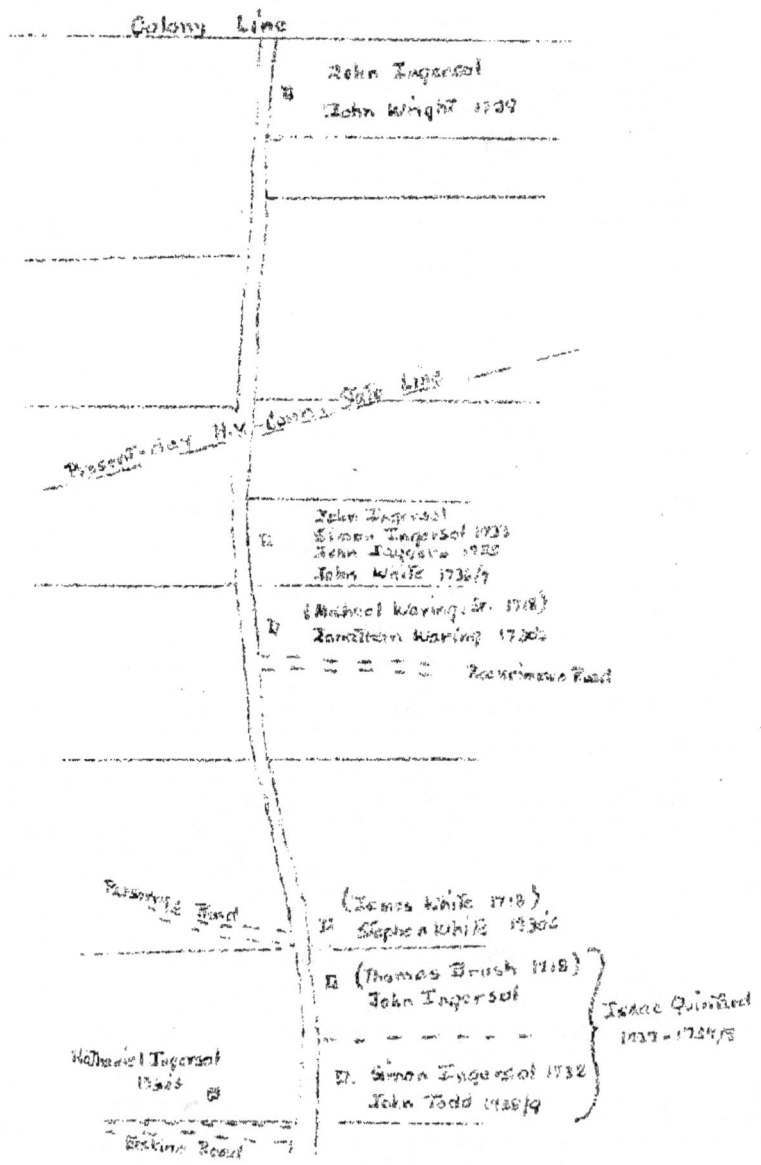

Colony Line

B   John Ingersol
    John Wright 1739

Present-day N.Y. - Conn. State Line

E   John Ingersol
    Simon Ingersol 1733
    John Ingersol 1738
    John Waite 1736/9

D   (Mahuel Waring, Sr. 1718)
    Jonathan Waring 1730's

                    Poorhouse Road

Purdy's Road

    (James White 1718)
D   Stephen White 1730's

E   (Thomas Brush 1718)   } Isaac Quinard
    John Ingersol   } 1733 - 1754/5

Nathaniel Ingersol   D   Simon Ingersol 1732
    1730's   John Todd 1738/9

Erskine Road

16

The younger Whites too were beginning to grow
up and to find their own places in Long Ridge. Stephen White, who was married in 1730, had a home on
the east of Bedford Road above Sam Ingersol's and on
the White land.[34] Quite possibly it was his father's
house. John White bought the Ingersol house from
John Jaggers in 1736; [35] he lived there until he
could build his own house on White land in the middle
tract on the west.

The only newcomer to the scene during this dec-
ade was John Todd of Branford, Connecticut. He
bought Simon's new house in 1738.[36] He may very
well have helped with the saw mill which the Ingersols probably had and in which John White had an interest.[37] The Ingersols themselves soon moved away
to Greenwich and the western part of Stamford, except for Samuel, who had considerable holdings and
was beginning his large family of six girls and two
sons. (Josiah, the youngest Ingersol son, did stay
in the area for a little longer than the rest.)

It may seem as though the inhabitants of Long
Ridge would have had little to do with the governing
body eight miles away in Stamford. However, they
were, as we have seen, useful in overseeing their
own area. Each able-bodied man took his turn at being a surveyor, for example. Stephen and John White;
Nathaniel, Simon, and Samuel Ingersol; and lastly,
John Todd in 1739 took their turns during this dec-
ade. Stephen and John White were also tithing men
(collecting the church tax), and John White and Si-

mon Ingersol were listers in 1739 and 1738 respectively. A lister had to list each man's estate and
present it in good form. Stephen was chosen as a
grand jury man in 1736.[38]

The 1740's were not kind to the White family,
for several members died. The remaining twin, John,
died in 1745 when he was thirty-six. His will, written in June of that year, mentions his increasing
sickness; he leaves his estate to his wife Jemima
and to his children, John, Jr., Sarah and Jemima, who
was destined to die soon also. John's inventory,
drawn up in part by his elder brother Stephen, gives
one a glimpse into the lives of these rather ordinary
farmers.[39] John was doing very well for himself
with about 50 acres of land, 7 cows and a bull, 2
horses, 5 pigs, and 3 hives of bees. This was about
the norm for a farmer of those times in Stamford, although often he would own a team of oxen. From John
White's possessions one can judge several things. He
was used to working in leather - saddles, bridles and
halters. Irons were important to his household: so
too were the churn and the two spinning wheels with
which to weave their cloth. The family lived rather
well with the luxuries of chocolate, spices, and sugar. They had adequate cooking and eating equipment
with a teapot and bowls and cups, pewter, tin, earth-
en and stoneware, knives and forks (the spoons must
have been forgotten!). Woolen sheets and linen sheets
and tablecloths were ample in number, and his list of
clothes marks him as a man of some means. The plush

16

breeches, wig, watch, glasses, neckbands, and shoes
with buckles show us a man dressed in his best. As
well as looking their best for church affairs, no
doubt these people found opportunities for social
functions. Travellers may well have visited as they
passed by along the Bedford Road.

The Inventory of John White's Estate

House and home lot
Barn and lot
Meadow Ridge lot
Lot west of Josiah Ingersol's house
Right in Boggy Meadow and in undivided land
Part of a saw mill with saw mill irons
Sawn boards   one mare   one horse
one pair of steers   four cows   one bull
one heifer   three calves   five swine
one ox yoke and chains   old iron
grain in barn   Indian corn   one hoe
saddle and bridle and leathern halter
two old saddles and an old bridle
two side saddles
two guns   saddler's tools   leather
two tramils   one pole and tongues
one pair hand irons   one box iron and heaters
one iron pot and kettle   one brass kettle and skillet
one pair hand bellows   one pair stillyards
one pair scales and weights   one frying pan
a warming pan   the pewterware
the tin ware   the earthen and stone ware
one teapot, cups and bowls, an hourglass and other
    glasses
chocolate, sugar and spice   two stone jugs and a jar
a cafe of bottles   two wheels and pair of cards and
    a hackle
wool and tow   barrels, hogsheads and cider
dry casks   pails and bucket
1/2 bushel and five trays and sifters
a brass tap   a brass ink bottle   knives and forks
one desk   one round table   two square tables
one chest   two old chests   one chest with drawers
one trunk   sixteen chairs   three looking glasses

two candlesticks   two pair of shears and one sheep-
  skin

sundry small things   thread, needles and brace but-
  tons

one testament   six bags   1/2 a grindstone   one
  churn

the bed in the chamber   bedstead covering and furniture

the bed in the out room   bedstead covering and furniture

the bed in the bedroom   bedstead covering and furniture

a trundle bedstead   six pair of sheets linen

six pair pillowcases   six tablecloths   six napkins

four towels   three hives of bees

four pair of woolen sheets   a strainer   one chop-
  ping knife

wearing apparel:

  a loose coat   a broadcloth coat and jacket

  a dowray coat and jacket   a broadcloth jacket

  a pair of plush breeches   a pair of leathern bree-
    ches

  a pair of russet breeches   a watch   a pair of
    glasses

  two linen jackets and a pair of linen breeches

  five shirts

  three neck bands   a hat and wig   gloves and cap

  five pair of stockings   shoes and buckles   one
    old hat

                    Jonathan Newman and Stephen White
                    October 30, 1745

                  * * * * * * * * * * * *

     John's brothers, Peter and Israel, moved to Nor-
walk and Danbury, and his sister married Augustine
Bryan of Huntington, Long Island. His half-brothers
were married in the 1740's: Timothy to Mary Newman
in 1740, and Jacob to Abigail Lounsbury in 1747. Timothy bought the Ingersol house from his brother

John,[40] and Jacob built his house on the White land to the west of the road sometime before 1750 when his brothers quit-claimed the tract to him.[41]

The Waring family during the '30's and '40's had been growing up. Jonathan, the oldest, married Mary Richards in 1736, and by 1746 they had a good start on their large family with five boys and a girl, one child about every two years. In 1745 Michael, the third son, was married, to be followed by Scudder the year after. The time had come to divide up the family lands.[42] Scudder, the second son, received 100 acres on the west of Bedford road, part of which was now recognized as being in New York; he also received a half of the undivided meadows well to the east and also partly in New York. Michael received a half of the homestead, Jonathan himself keeping the northern part. He also received the other half of the undivided and 40 acres to the southwest of Scudder. It is not clear who received their father's house, but Jonathan probably did, though he must have expanded it to meet the needs of his ever-growing household. Jonathan kept for himself the Boggy Meadow to the east and about 60 acres south of Scudder's tract.

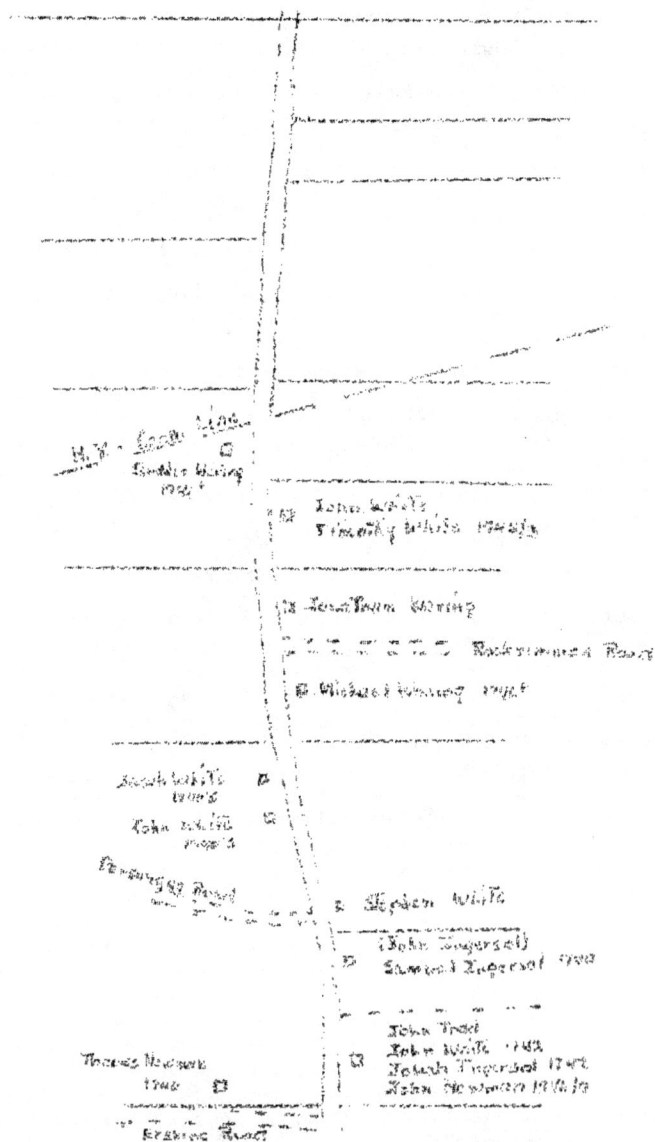

Long Ridge in the 1740's

22

In 1746 also, a new person joined the seven or eight families. This was John Newman, who bought Josiah Ingersol's house.[43] It had been Simon's house originally and later was John Todd's. John Todd had left Long Ridge in 1742, presumably for North Castle. John Newman was not really new to the area since his family had lived at Larance's Farm for many years and relatives lived along the Stanwich road between Long Ridge and Stanwich.

Probably he took over Josiah's interest in the saw mill. This mill had evidently played its part the year before, for in the town records for December 24, 1745 Timothy White and Josiah were given the assignment "to build a pound and set it where the old pound stands." They were to make the rails of chestnut and the posts of "oke".[44] Was this in Pound Ridge which is known to have had a pound since the Indian days?[45] The job was to be done by May 1, and they were to receive £ 25.

Both Stephen White and Timothy were active in the town's affairs during the 1740's. Stephen was a tithing man and a surveyor until 1742 when "Lieutenant Stephen White" was excused and Jonathan Waring took his place. Timothy was a grand jury man in 1744, a lister in 1746, and a surveyor in 1749. Scudder Waring, Josiah Ingersol, and Samuel Ingersol also took over jobs as town viewer, surveyor, and lister.[46] A town viewer had the duty of checking every homeowner's fences so that animals could not roam at large and cause havoc to growing crops and vegetable gardens.

This use of all men who were dependable for the necessary tasks of town government was of rather remarkable value. Men took their duties seriously and felt challenged to live up to the respect accorded them. They also gained a spirit of oneness in that they did have to report their business to the town at meeting time and so were able to hear of the problems of others, to learn of the affairs of the town, to gain some ideas of their own. Later they would report back to those in the home community over a pipe and a mug of cider. The dissemination of ideas and the passing on of correct forms of discussion and problem-solving helped to make men sturdy, sober thinkers and careful, practical organizers. When the American Revolution came to New England with its resultant new government, the methods used in the town governments were to prove of great positive value.

By 1750 Long Ridge Village was a flourishing community of nine families, consisting of between 50 and 60 persons. The list below gives the names of the second-generation homeowners, when they were married, and approximately the numbers in their households:

Stephen White (1730)	10	
John White, d. (1733)	3 or 4	
Timothy White (1740)	6	
Jacob White (1747)	3	
Samuel Ingersol (1735)	6	
Jonathan Waring (1736)	9	
Scudder Waring (1746)	3	
Michael Waring (1745)	4	
John Newman (c. 1730)	6	

There probably were various unmarried women living with their relatives and some hired help as well.

What can be seen today in Long Ridge of the community as it was in the first half of the eighteenth century aside from the main road, the innumerable stone walls, and the rolling farm lands of fields, marshes, rivers, and ponds? Not much. Some of the early driftways (an English term used for paths that cattle were driven along) used by the farmers to get to their back lands are still in use today. Parsonage Road, which dips down from Old Long Ridge Road and crosses the new Long Ridge road is truly an innocent little track, which the early Whites would have no trouble at all in recognizing. Rockrimmon Road probably began as a driftroad between Jonathan Waring's and Michael Waring's homesteads as a way to get to the "Great Meadows" beyond. A few houses of this period do exist but in much changed form. Jacob White's house, built on White land to the west of Bedford Road, is embedded in a much grander house today, though its simple facade right on the road allows one to recognize the early house. John White's house just south of it seems to have gone, although an old house does occupy the same spot. Opposite Jacob's house were the Whites' barns and cowsheds, etc., and now an early nineteenth-century house, built by later Whites on the pattern of the eighteenth-century homes, is one of the best preserved of its style in the area. Stephen White's house might possibly be traced not far from what is probably his barn - a

25

beautifully built structure with the numbers on its
beams still visible today and a justly cherished
showpiece of Long Ridge. Samuel Ingersol's house,
probably his second one built about 1756, according
to Frederick Ayres' diary, is on the east side below
where Stephen's was. It has been enlarged and has a
second floor on it as it didn't originally. And,
lastly, Scudder Waring's and his son Joseph's house
to the west of the road and just below the New York
line also may exist in part of the large house there
today.

The second half of the eighteenth century witnessed gradual growth to Long Ridge Village, but a noticeable change in the balance occurs. The Whites and the
Ingersols move away or die, and the Warings, thanks
mainly to Jonathan, take over much of the community.
Jonathan's children were as follows: James (1736),
Michael (1738), Jonathan (1740), Samuel (1743), Rebecca (1744), Joel (1746), Jesse (1748), Elizabeth
(1751), Abraham (1753), Mary (1755), Noah (1757),
James (1759), and Abigail (1761), making thirteen in
all. Jonathan not only was busy with his own family,
but also must have had some responsibility for his
younger brother Michael's family, for Michael died
in 1755, leaving five children (the oldest only 10)
and one posthumous son. Michael's home was just
south of Jonathan's, conveniently close. Scudder,
the other brother, had two growing sons, Joseph and
Ebenezer.

The other two families were decreasing in numb-

26

ers. The Whites were now represented by only Stephen and Jacob, as Timothy moved away, selling his house and 19 acres to Jonathan Waring.[47] The Ingersols were represented by Samuel's family only.

The five men, Jonathan, Scudder, Samuel, Jacob, and Stephen took turns at the usual jobs handed out by the Stamford town meetings. It is interesting to note that by 1756 Stephen is referred to as Captain Stephen White and Jonathan is Sergeant Jonathan Waring. Captain Stephen occupied the grand position of selectman, which Jonathan also held later.[48] Jonathan in 1752-53 was probably responsible for the laying out of what is now called Erskine Road, for in 1753 surveyors were sent out to see about the advisability of a road from Larance's Farm to Long Ridge.[49] In 1760 James Hait, who lived to the south of Long Ridge village, gave up land for a highway to run from Bedford Road just "4 rods south of Selleck's old line."[50] Before this there were references to a path going from Long Ridge to Stanwich - a well-beaten path it must have been.

It would be interesting to know a little more about the various occupations these men had besides their farming because, over the years, a man might well develop a skill at a profit to himself and of benefit to his neighbors. A farmer in those days, by force of circumstance, had to operate on a self-sufficient scale. The inventories offer evidence that a farmer could handle all the needs of his animals, grow his crops and garden produce, construct his buildings, and supply his own tool and gear needs for the most part. He also had to provide the winter fuel. Even today there are some mysterious large, dark circles in the ground where little will grow; inhabitants of Long Ridge wonder if they go back to the Indian days. But no, these were the charcoal pits where the farmers burned big stacks of wood down to the charcoal stage.[51] Some jobs the women could help with; meat was salted down, fruits and vegetables stored in special root cellars or under the barn or house, soap was made. Then the woman had her special tasks; in addition to feeding her family and caring for the home, she made the clothes. The inventories list different kinds of spinning wheels for spinning the tow and wool; some include looms. Then too there are cheese presses and cider barrels and bee hives (useful for both honey and wax for candles). It is of small wonder that hardly a book appears in the inventories of this time.

Besides the essential millers for the saw and grist mills other specialists needed by a community were: a blacksmith, a currier and a sadler, a cooper, or barrel and basket maker, carpenters, a shopkeeper or two, a tailor and a shoemaker. Professional men were needed too, such as a minister, a doctor, a schoolteacher. Unfortunately, though, one can tell little about what was happening in this direction until the tax lists beginning in 1785 note the essential occupations in Stamford. We do see, though, a few suggestions earlier: John White must have had

some skill with leather; Timothy White and Josiah
Ingersol were good at carpentry. With the coming of
age of Ezra Newman, John's son, in the 1760's we do
find a definite trade existing in Long Ridge Village.
He was listed twenty years later as both a silversmith and a blacksmith,[52] and when his inventory was
made by Jonathan and Joel Waring at the end of the
century, he owned "part of an old blacksmith's shop,
3 small blacksmith's hammers, a lot of tools of pin-
chers and punchers, an old anvil, an old vise", and
an "old pair of blacksmith's bellows". He did, of
course, have his animals and crops but couldn't have
been very well off. Only one set of clothes, consisting of a coat, a waistcoat, breeches, and a hat
seemed to be worthy of mention.[53]

In 1763 a young man returned to Long Ridge. John
Todd, Jr. of North Castle bought 105 acres to the
west of Bedford Road (along Erskine Road today).[54] In
1771 he bought another 3 acres of Ezra to the south
of Ezra's house on the east of Bedford Road and began
the reign of the Todds over the saw and grist mills
situated on the millponds below.[55] Both Ezra and he
were living on land that had belonged to the Daven-
ports and was southerly from the original Long Ridge.
Todd's mills were extremely successful so that each
of John's sons, John, Noah, Elnathan, and Washington,
was given a good start in life. John's sawmill was
left to John 3 and Noah together.[56]

A doctor , Dr. John Wilson, bought land in Long
Ridge in 1770,[57] although it is uncertain that he,

as an important figure in Stamford, spent much time
at his farm. He bought all of Captain White's lands
and his dwelling house north of Samuel Ingersol's,
and for some time there were Wilsons living in Long
Ridge. Stephen's son, Stephen, who married a Quintard girl, moved to Rome, New York, where he was a
doctor.[58]

Another White family to move out of Long Ridge
was John White's. They sold their lands partly to
their uncle Jacob and partly to Jonathan Waring, who
acquired 50 acres.[59]

For some years Jonathan had been amassing land
as well as several houses. Five of his children had
been married by 1770, and he evidently settled some
of them in houses on his own lands without bothering
about deeds. It is difficult, therefore, to trace
the affairs of three of the four oldest living sons
as there is little on record about them. Jonathan
and Mary had their last child, Abigail, in 1761 when
they were grandparents as well. Jonathan, Jr. was em-
ulating his father, for by 1770 he had five children,
one born every other year; Michael, who had died,
probably had one son; Samuel had three, and Joel, the
sixth child, had Joel, Jr. Rebecca Waring had done
well for herself in marrying Dr. Stephen Rockwell,
well known in Stamford, and for awhile they too re-
sided in Long Ridge.

Jonathan, a member of the church at Stanwich
and later to be a deacon,[60] a position of some honor,

was also increasingly busy with town affairs. He
was both a grand jury man and a town viewer in 1760
and was a surveyor and a viewer several times thereafter. In 1765 he was appointed to gather the rate
of one penny and to be paid £ 3/65 for his service.
His two sons, Jonathan and Samuel, began their duties
as surveyors, and Jonathan, Jr. also became a grand
jury man and a viewer. All the men of Long Ridge were
represented on the town list of officials as the need
arose for more men to cover the expanding territory.
John Todd and Ezra Newman were grand jury men, John
Newman and Scudder Waring, surveyors, and Captain
Stephen White appeared on the list for the last time
in 1762 as grand jury man.[61]

As the time for the American War for Independ-
ence approached, Long Ridge Village united in its at-
titude towards the British. No one appears to have
had Loyalist sympathies. Jonathan Waring, Jr., who
had followed his father in collecting the tax and had
received a remuneration of £ 4 in 1773,[62] also served
on a committee to show its acceptance of the 11th Article of the Congress (the First Continental Congress,
which drew up a list of grievances against England
and recommended a boycott against British trade).[63]
In 1775 he was again on the Congress Committee (in con-
nection with the Second Continental Congress), and in
1776 he was on a committee set up to take care of the
families who were suffering because of the war.[64] In
1777 a number of the Long Ridge men took the Oath of
Fidelity. Samuel Waring, Ezra Newman, Jonathan Waring,

Jr., Jesse Waring, John Newman, Libbeus White, and
Ebenezer Waring.[65] This seems to be a rather odd
list, for others of equal stature, such as Jonathan
Waring, John Todd, Joseph Waring, are not included
though they certainly were patriots. Conceivably,
they were away at the war at the time.

All the men of Long Ridge Village went forth to
fight for the cause. The surprising element that one
notes about their service is that often the time was
so very short. However, men could be called only for
a period of three months. Some men returned home after a few days only. The following chart covers the
activities of the Long Ridge men as well as can be as-
certained.[66] The numbers show the months of service;
the stars, indeterminate period or whole years.

	1775	1776	1777	1778	1779	1780 and on	
Waring							
Abraham		6	1	*			lieutenant
Ebenezer			2				
James		6	*	*	*	*	a pensioner
Jesse		1,2	*				corporal
John	6						sergeant
Jonathan						*	captain
Jonathan					*		
Joseph		2	*		*	*	sergeant
Noah		2					
Samuel		2					
Scudder				1		9 *	
White							
Jacob				8			
Jacob, Jr						*	
Libbeus		*					
Ingersol							
Samuel		3					

32

1775 1776 1777 1778 1779 1780 and on

Newman
  Ezra   1

Todd   sergeant and
  John   3   drummer

When John Todd died in the 1800's, his inventory included a number of music books.[67]

Life back at home in Long Ridge was not so calm.
Although the community seemed so far from any important scene of activity, nevertheless the British army
approached all too close when General Tarleton marched
on Pound Ridge in 1779.[68]   Fortunately that raid was
diverted, but the Britishers did remain in the area
and foraged for animals to replenish their supplies.
In Long Ridge various animals were seized and carried
off.   The farmers thereafter presented their claims
in order to receive compensation, chiefly abatements
in their taxes.   Dr. John Wilson lost 2 cows, Ebenezer and Joseph Waring 8 cows and 2 oxen.   John Todd
lost two pair of oxen and 5 cows.   Jacob White lost
4 horses, Jesse Waring lost 3 horses, and Joseph Waring lost 6 cows, one pair of oxen, and a one-year-old.
All these losses occurred between 1780 and July of
1782.[69]

Washington's army also took an interest in
Long Ridge Village and, in its 1778 map of Stamford,
included Long Ridge with the houses of most of the
occupants labelled.   This map has proved to be very
exact and is valuable in pin-pointing the eighteenth-century houses that exist today.

33

A SECTION OF

THE ERSKINE MAP OF 1778

made for George Washington

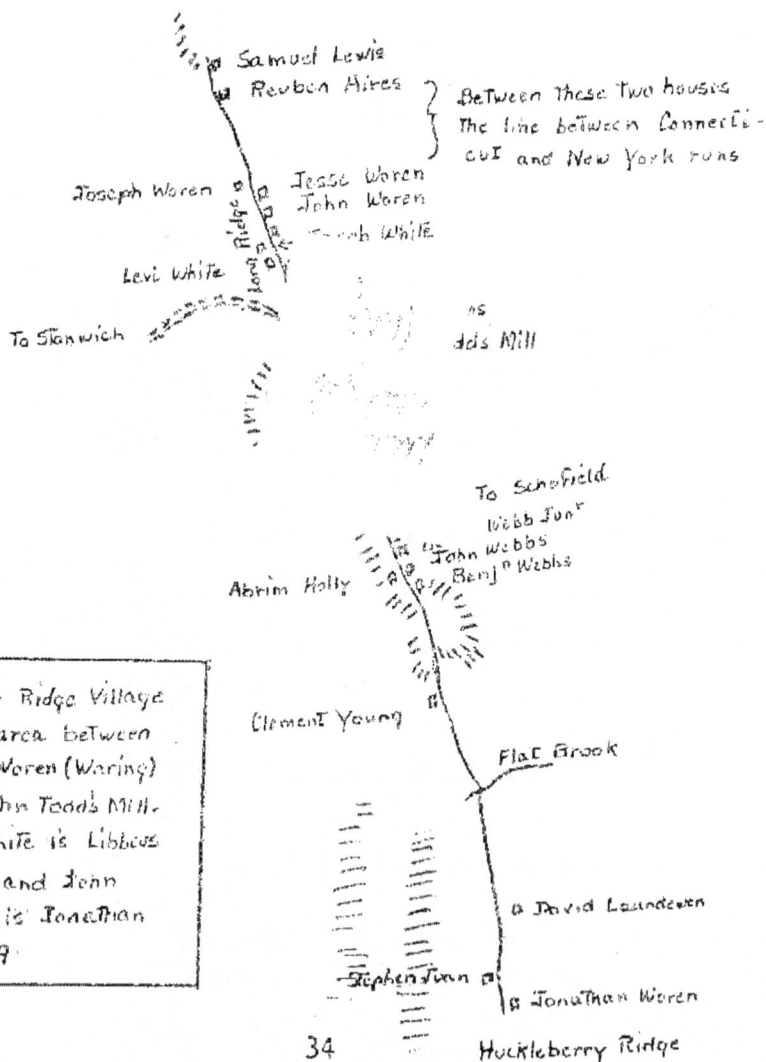

Samuel Lewis
Reuben Aires

Between these two houses
The line between Connecticut and New York runs

Joseph Woren

Jesse Woren
John Woren
Joseph White

Levi White

To Stanwich

dds Mill

To Schofield
Webb Junr
John Webbs
Benjn Webbs

Abrim Holly

Clement Young

Flat Brook

David Laundeven

Stephen Ivan

Jonathan Woren

34

Huckleberry Ridge

The Long Ridge Village
is the area between
Joseph Woren (Waring)
and John Todd's Mill.
Levi White is Libbeus
White, and John
Woren is Jonathan
Woring.

At the end of the 1770's two well known inhabitants of Long Ridge came to the end of their lives: Scudder Waring in 1777, and Jacob White's oldest son, Libbeus, in 1779. Scudder was only 52; he left his wife Martha and their two sons, Joseph and Ebenezer, who were in their middle twenties, to carry on the homestead of 9 acres and the extensive farm lands they were already in possession of. Scudder's inventory shows that he had a small shop, a parcel of shoe molds and lasts, awl blades, and sole leather. He must have enjoyed shoemaking as well as caring for his farm. He had kept his animals: 5 horses, a pair of oxen, 12 head of cattle, 18 sheep, and four skips of bees. Some objects he owned are interesting, such as a gun and a sword, a beaver hat, spectacles, several books including a pocket dictionary and "Common Sense with an appendix." He also had three night caps.[70] The younger son Ebenezer soon released his half of the house to Joseph who lived there until he was an old man.[71]

Libbeus' death was a real tragedy as he was drowned[72] when only 31 and had three very young children. Israel, who was only about a year old at the time, grew up to be a goldsmith. The inventory of Libbeus' estate shows possessions that are typical of a man of his age and time; he too owned a beaver hat!

How many families were living in Long Ridge Village by the end of the war in 1781, and what had changed in their lives?

The Samuel Ingersol family seems to have fallen

upon hard times in the 1770's and 1780's. Of the two
sons, Benjamin died in 1776, leaving a wife (Mercy
Webster) and two children, John and Polly, after only
three years of marriage. In the same year Samuel, Jr.
received most of his father's land on the west side
of Bedford Road, including a house on the north corner of the road to Stanwich,[73] but he enjoyed the 89
acres for only a short time and had to sell it all to
a Richard Titus of Purchase, N.Y. [74] (The house,
though, on 4 acres of land went to John Todd, Jr. in
1784).[75] After Samuel Ingersol, Sr. died in 1788,
Elizabeth and her children stayed in the family home
for a year, and then they sold the homestead of 20
acres to Aaron Stuart, who had previously bought the
old Stephen White house to the north.[76] Aaron Stuart is listed in the tax list for 1790 as an innkeep-
er. Did he turn this house into an inn for Long Ridge
for a few years?

The second and third sons of the Jacob White
family had reached marriageable age. Jacob and his
wife Abigail were now grandparents, particularly concerned about Libbeus's young family, whose home bor-
dered theirs on the south. Along with the lands and
house given to Libbeus, they had been allotting par-
cels to the other two sons. In 1781 Jacob, Jr. was
yet unmarried but was evidently planning on his marriage to Esther Hait, for his father gave him 60 acres
and a new house well down on the south side of the
road leading to Stanwich.[77] In the same year Jacob,
Sr. gave his youngest son, William, a half of his own

36

house and 60 acres.[78]   William, married to Susannah
Smith, lost his first son William during the year but
had another son the same year and gave him the same
name. Their later life was rather troubled as they
lost three more of their two succeeding children. Both
Jacob, Jr.'s and William's families remained in the
Long Ridge area for many years, some descendants even
into the 1920's.

It is hard to determine whether at that time
sons of the Warings belonged to the Pound Ridge community in New York or the Stanwich-Long Ridge community. The family of Jonathan's youngest brother, Michael, did move into Pound Ridge, principally because
most of their father's land was there and because
their mother Sally had married Jonathan Weeks, a resident there. The son John had remained in the family
home, but after his death in 1775, the wife and brothers sold the lands in Long Ridge and the house to
their cousin, Joseph Waring. He promptly sold the
house and 14 acres to Jonathan Waring.[79]

Joseph Waring also owned lands in both Pound
Ridge and Long Ridge. He had considerable holdings
and became quite wealthy - taxed for over £ 2000 in
Pound Ridge alone.[80]   He and his wife Abigail White,
had no sons, only Martha and Abigail, though he later served as guardian for Scudder, his brother Ebenezer's son. He also had two children by his second
wife whom he married in 1780.

Jonathan Waring owned several hundred acres of

37

land, some in Bedford, some in Pound Ridge, and some
in Stamford. He was very circumspect about his land
dealings and also about the several houses that he
acquired, such as the one from Timothy White and that
of his brother Michael. Undoubtedly, as his sons married, he set them up in homes, but then as some of
them died, he shuffled the homes about, all without
making any formal deeds. It will be enough for the
purpose of this essay to show how at the end of his
life his lands had been apportioned:[81]

To Jonathan, Jr.	10-1/4 acres	1765
Jesse	5 acres and a house	1774
Jonathan, Jr.	111 acres and 1/2 a house	1778
Abraham	111 acres and 1/2 a house	1778
Hezron (son of Samuel)	13 acres and a house	1791
Joel's sons	a farm in Bedford	1793
James	119 acres and a house	1801
Noah's heirs	100 acres and a house	1801
Jesse's heirs	124 acres	1801

Jonathan, Jr.'s and Abraham's house was south of Long
Ridge at the beginning of Hunting Ridge, which was
called Huckleberry Ridge then. Hezron's house, on
the land where Simon Ingersol once lived, exists today; half of it seems to have been a shop of some
kind. As Jotham, Hezron's brother, was a blacksmith
and also lived there, he may have used it. Jesse's
house, which also exists today and has a cornerstone
marked "J.W. 1779", is particularly interesting because in the deed Jonathan states that he is giving
the house "a part of which I built". The house has,
of course, been changed considerably and the southern

half has been added on, but enough of the old structure is visible so that one can reasonably say, "Jonathan may have shaped that." His own house he gave
to Noah, his grandchild, who was only five. He seems
to have been particularly fond of his son Noah's second wife and family.

Ezra Newman, the blacksmith, quite often held
positions of importance during the 1780's. He served
in 1780 as inspector of provisions and later as grand
jury man and as surveyor.[82]

Long Ridge Village can be fully substantiated as
to its inhabitants in 1790 when the first census was
made.[83] The names in the order they appear on it are
as follows:

> John Todd
> Richard Sibley
> Ezra Newman
>
> Elisabeth Ingersol (wd.)
> Aaron Stuart
> Gershom Lockwood
> Lines Waring
> Stephen Rockwell
> Jacob White
> William White
> Jonathan Waring
> Jesse Waring
> Joseph Waring
> Noah Waring

(Jacob White Jr. is, of course, on the list, but he
lived too far down the Stanwich road to be included
in the village itself.) One notes the route of the
census-taker to be along the Stanwich road first and
and then from there north.

There were at that time 73 people living in
Long Ridge Village and the community was becoming a
thriving, well organized little center. There appear
on the census list only four new names. Richard Sibley moved into the village in 1785 when he bought
from John Todd the little Ingersol tract with a house
on it that was on the north corner of the road to
Stanwich.[84]   With him he brought a useful skill, for
he is listed in the tax lists as a tailor. Gershom
Lockwood occupied the house where Aaron Stuart dwelt.
He wasn't there for long, though, and must have rented, for in 1796 Jonathan Waring, who had bought it
from Stuart, sold it with its little south garden and
well to Nathan Wilson.[85]   Linas Waring is a bit of a
mystery as he appears only on this list, on the tax
list for 1790, and in Jonathan Waring's will in 1804.
It is possible that he was the son of Samuel by his
first wife, Sarah Hait.

In the 1790's proper business companies appeared
in Long Ridge Village. Ezra Newman organized a blacksmith company, which probably included his son-in-law
Joel Waring, as he is listed in the tax list as a
blacksmith. William White is listed as a merchant and
had a company. John Todd 3 formed a company of join-
ers and carpenters, and Noah Todd, who made Jonathan
Waring's coffin,[86] must have worked with him. The
two Todd sons, Noah and John 3, did very well with
their work and with the saw mill, for in 1793 they
bought 147 acres from John and James Davenport (sons
of Abraham).[87]   The land was to the east of Sawmill

40

Pond and Stony Brook and to the south of the village --
to below Mill Road as it is today. They also bought
Aaron Stuart's 50-acre tract with the large house,
which later became Washington Todd's home, and Hezron's
and Jotham's home, which became Elnathan's.[88]

Their father, John Todd, had a certain concern
for his friends in the community at the time Ezra Newman died. He responded in May 1797 by donating a
piece of land 12 rods square for a cemetery.[89]   It
was north and east of Frederick Hoyt's little house on
the road to Stanwich. (This little red house has remained remarkably unchanged since it was built about
1775; it stands on a small knoll to the north of the
road.) The original cemetery was placed 16 rods from
the road and was to be for the benefit of the following people: John's four sons, Ezra Newman, the first
to be buried there, Jeremiah Knapp, who had bought the
land of William Titus and lived at the end of Parsonage Road,[90]   and Frederick Hoyt. John Todd, who died
in 1814, was remembered on his tombstone with the following poem, barely legible today --

> I gave my friends this burying ground
> To rest till the last Trump shall sound.
> May we all then in triumph rise
> To meet our Saviour in the skies.

There were, of course, other cemeteries, family
ones, in the area, such as the Waring one near the Colony Line, now destroyed,[91] but this one was the fore-
runner of a true community cemetery, and it exists,
many times expanded, as Long Ridge Cemetery today.

The beginning of the nineteenth century saw a
pleasant community of just under 100 persons at Long
Ridge, and it saw, too, the passing of the last two
members of the second generation of settlers. Jacob
White died in 1799 at the age of 73, his last two
years saddened by the death of his son Jacob at the
age of 41. Jonathan Waring, having watched the growth
of his little village over most of its history, was
living out his last years surrounded by children and
grandchildren. He outlived six of his sons, only Jonathan, Jr., Abraham, and James surviving him, but in
spite of the anxiety and sorrows, he had lived a tre-
mendously full life and had done well for all of his
relatives and friends. His will, written in 1804,[92]
is a carefully particularized document, exactly what
one would expect of such a man. It is signed in the
wavering writing of an old man, but the writing is
legible and forceful notwithstanding. Jonathan died
after a week or two of illness in 1805. He had been
cared for by two of his daughters in the home of
Stephen Bishop, where he had become stricken. His inventory is of little account - a walking stick, a few
clothes, and bedding, etc. were all that remained of
this enterprising, hard-working, and tenacious man.

Those who are fortunate to live in Long Ridge
today have a precious heritage. The little settlement
is one of the few areas in and around Stamford to pre-
serve its early nature. Although the fight to keep
gaudy business, modern-style houses, and efficient
wide thoroughfares away is a fight that never ends,

42

it is to be hoped that Long Ridge Village will become
widely recognized by all for its unique background
and still evident charm and that it will be carefully
preserved for future generations to enjoy.

The Waring Family

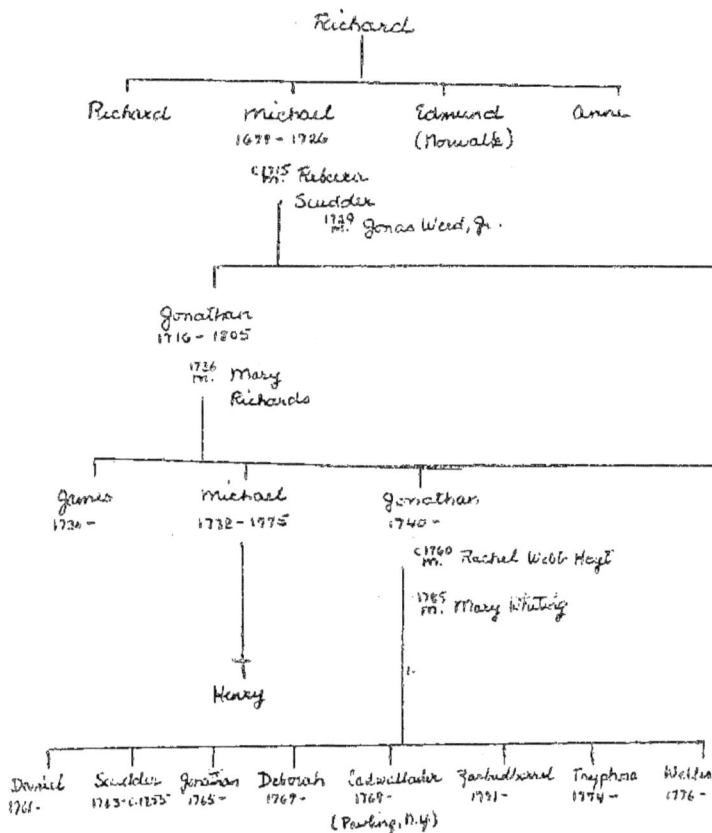

Richard

- Richard
- Michael
  1679 - 1726
  m. 1715 Rebecca Scudder
  m. 1719 Jonas Weed, Jr.
- Edmund
  (Norwalk)
- Anne

Jonathan
1716 - 1805
m. 1736 Mary Richards

- James
  1736 -
- Michael
  1732 - 1775

  Henry
- Jonathan
  1740 -
  m. <1760 Rachel Webb Hoyt
  m. 1765 Mary Whiting
  1.

  - Daniel
    1761 -
  - Scudder
    1763 - c.1253
  - Jonathan
    1765 -
  - Deborah
    1767 -
  - Cadwallader
    1769 -
    (Pawling, N.Y.)
  - Zarbudland
    1771 -
  - Tryphosa
    1774 -
  - Wellin
    1776 -

The Waring Family

Michael's children
_____

Jonathan's children
_____

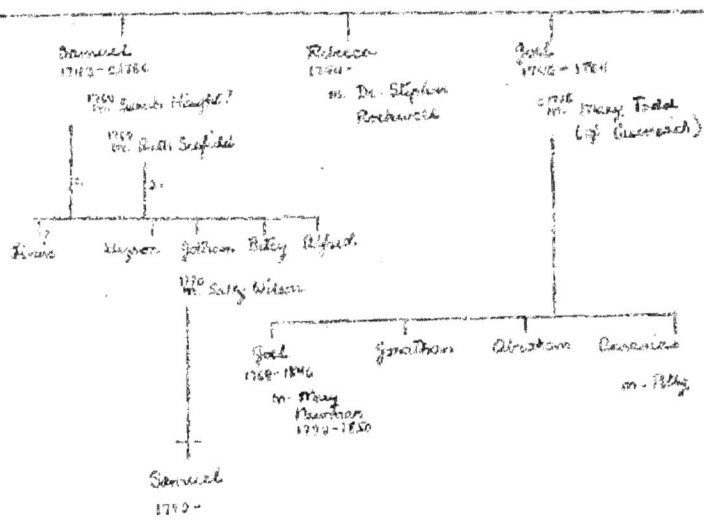

Samuel	Rebecca	Joel
1743 - c1786	1744 -	1746 - 1784
1769 m. Sarah Hempsted?	m. Dr. Stephen	c1778 m. Mary Todd
1772 m. Sarah Seafield	Rockwell	(of Greenwich)

Reuce   Abyjah   Jotham   Betsey   Alfred

1770 Sally Wilson

Joel	Jonathan	Abraham	Catherine
1769 - 1846			m. Filley
m. Mary			
Newman			
1772 - 1850			

Samuel
1790 -

The Waring Family

Michael's children

Jonathan's children

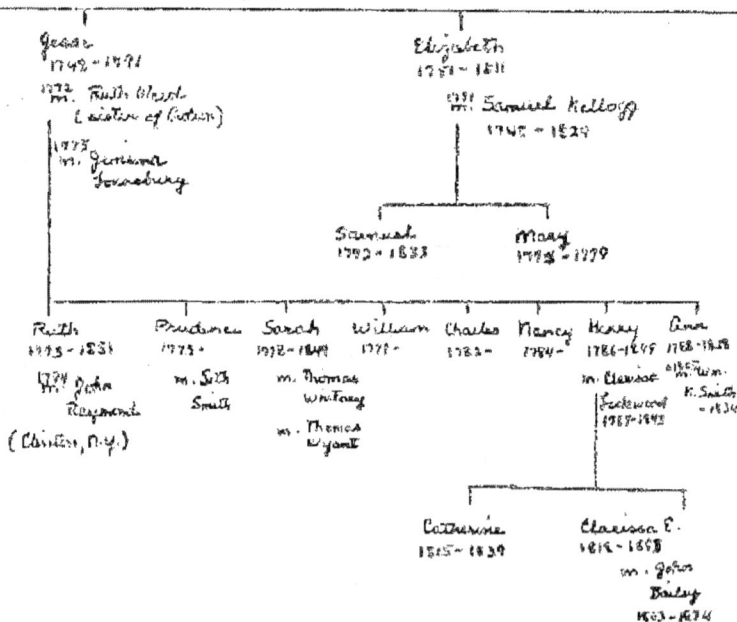

Jesse
1742 – 1791
1772 m. Ruth Wheat
(sister of Cotton)
1773 m. Jerusha
Tomsbury

Elizabeth
1751 – 1811
1771 m. Samuel Kellogg
1745 – 1829

Samuel
1772 – 1833

Mary
1774 – 1779

Ruth
1773 – 1831
1794 m. John
Raymond
(Clinton, N.Y.)

Prudence
1775 –
m. Seth
Smith

Sarah
1778 – 1849
m. Thomas
Whitney
m. Thomas
Wyant

William
1771 –

Charles
1782 –

Nancy
1784 –

Henry
1786 – 1849
m. Eleanor
Lockwood
1789 – 1843

Ann
1788 – 1858
1805 m.
Wm.
K. Smith
– 1834

Catherine
1815 – 1839

Clarissa E.
1818 – 1898
m. John
Bailey
1803 – 1874

46

The Waring Family

Michael's children

Jonathan's children

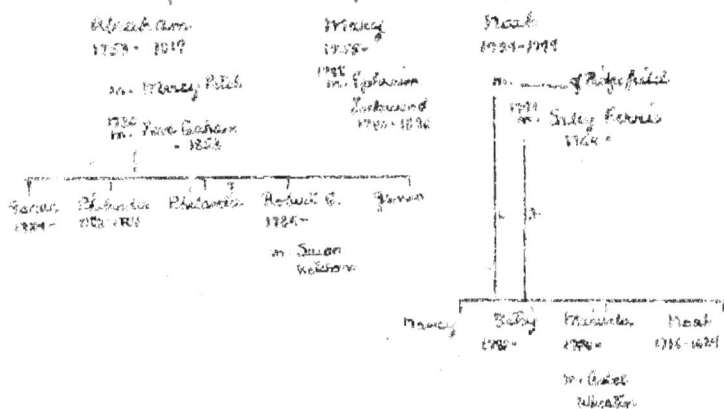

Abraham
1759 - 1817

m. Mercy Fitch

1796
m. Jane Graham
- 1834

Mercy
1765-

1798
m. Ephraim
Lockwood
1765-1856

Noah
1754-1799

m. _____ of Ridgefield

1791
m. Sibley Ferris
1768-

Gamu
1784-

Philander
1786-1795

Philander

Abiail E.
1794-

m. Susan
Weldham

Sarah

Mercy
1790-

Baby
1794-

Miranda
1794-

Noah
1796-1851

m. Aurel
Wheaton

The Waring Family

Michael's children

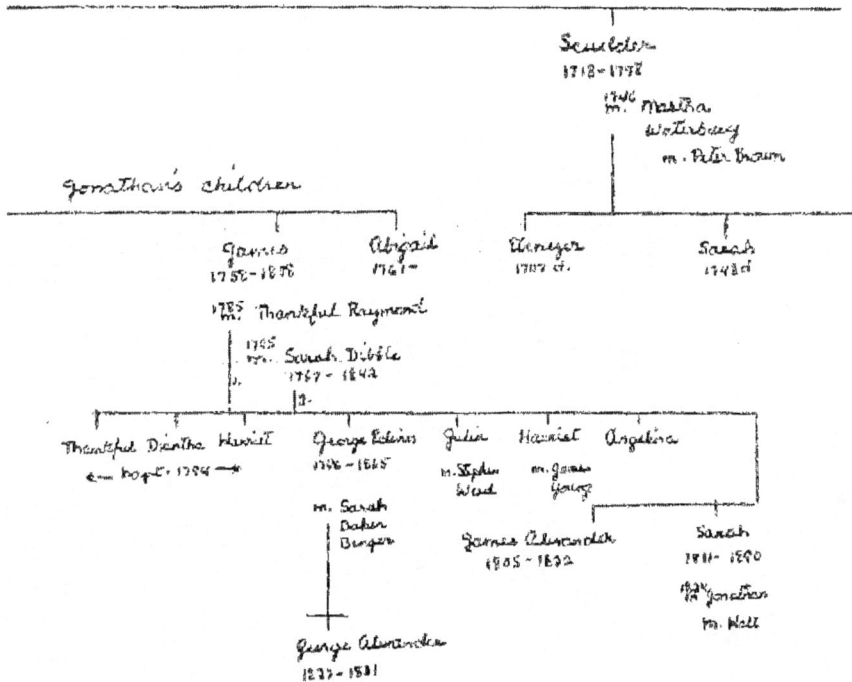

```
                                                    Scudder
                                                   1718-1798
                                                   1746
                                                   m. Martha
                                                      Waterbury
                                                      m. Peter Brown

Jonathan's children

        James        Abigail          Ebenezer        Sarah
       1758-1876      1761-            1787 d.         1748 d.
    1785
    m. Thankful Raymond
       1795
    m. Sarah Dibble
       1767-1842

Thankful Diantha Harriet    George Edwins    Julia      Harriet    Angelina
   b. bapt. 1794-           1796-1845       m. Stephen  m. James
                                               Wood        Young
                            m. Sarah
                               Baker          James Alexander      Sarah
                               Burger         1805-1832           1811-1890
                                                                  1834
                                                                  m. Jonathan
                            George Alexander                      m. Hall
                            1832-1831
```

The Waring Family

Michael's children

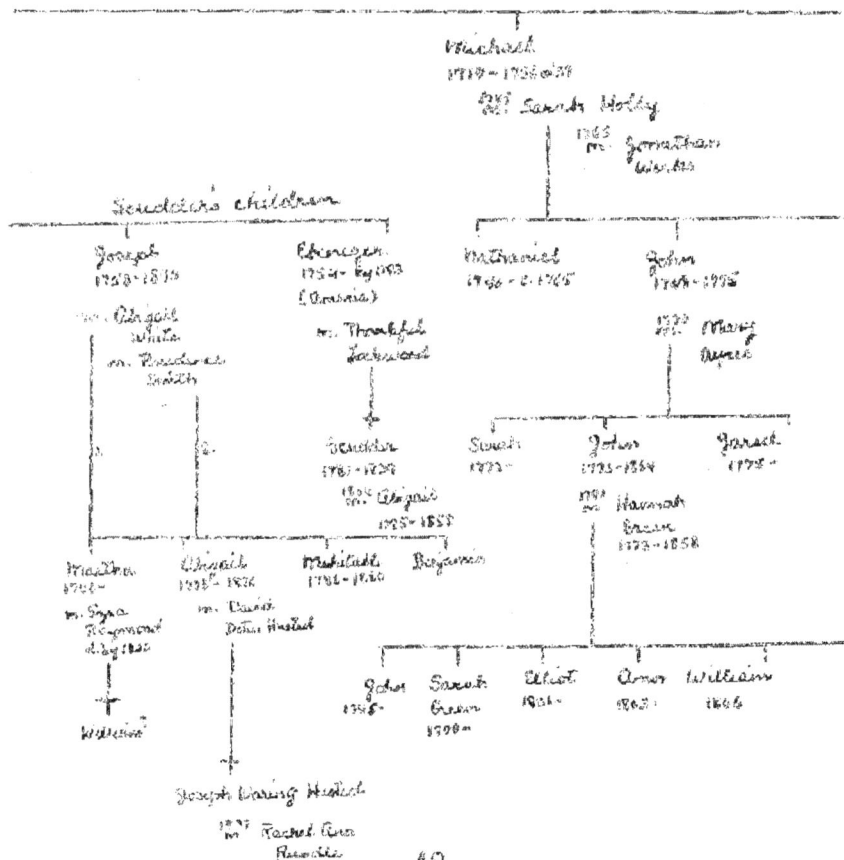

Michael
1719 - 1756 æ 39
2nd Sarah Moldy
1765
m. Jonathan
Waring

Scudder's children

Joseph
1753 - 1815
m. Abigail
White
m. Rachel
Smith

Ebenezer
1754 - Aug 1803
(Orasna)
m. Thankful
Lockwood

Nathaniel
1756 - c. 1765

John
1764 - 1775
1771
m. Mary
Ayres

Scudder
1787 - 1729
1808 Abigail
1785 - 1855

Sarah
1773 -

John
1775 - 1864
1791
m. Hannah
Green
1773 - 1858

Sarah
1775 -

Martha
1792 -
m. Sina
Raymond
d. Aug 1820

Orsrah
1798 - 1876
m. David
John Haslet

Matilda
1782 - 1820

Benjamin

John
1795 -

Sarah
Green
1790 -

Eliot
1804 -

Amos
1805 -

William
1806

William

Joseph Waring Haslet
1837
m. Rachel Ann
Randall

49

The Waring Family

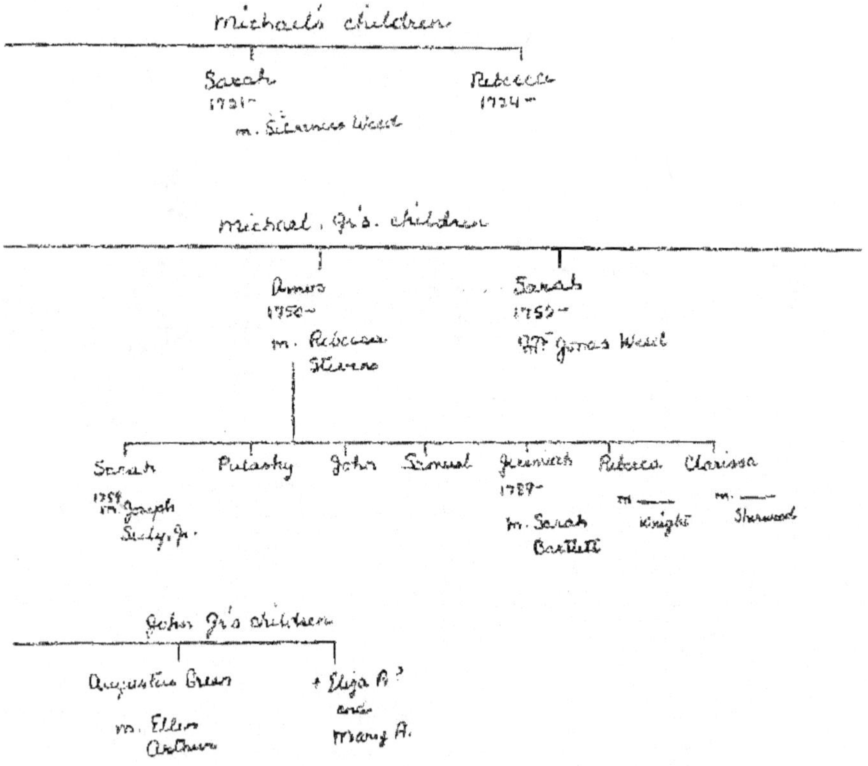

Michael's children

Sarah
1721-
m. Silvanus West

Rebecca
1724-

Michael, Jr's. children

Amos
1750-
m. Rebecca
Stevens

Sarah
1752-
m. Jonas West

Sarah
1758
m. Joseph
Sisty, Jr.

Pulaski

John

Samuel

Jerimiah
1789-
m. Sarah
Bartlett

Rebecca
m. Knight

Clarissa
m. Sherwood

John Jr's children

Augustus Green
m. Ellen
Arthur

+ Eliza B.?
and
Mary A.

50

The Waring Family

Michael, 9's children

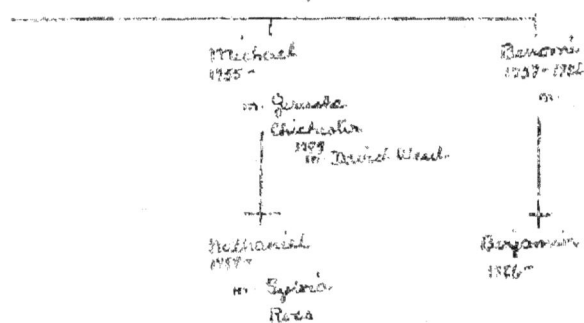

```
Michael                          Benconi
1955 ~                           1559 - 1784
                                    m.
  m. Jemima
     Chichester
        1279
     m. Daniel Weak


  Nathaniel                      Benjamin
  1757 ~                         1566 ~
   m. Sophia
      Ross
```

51

The White Family

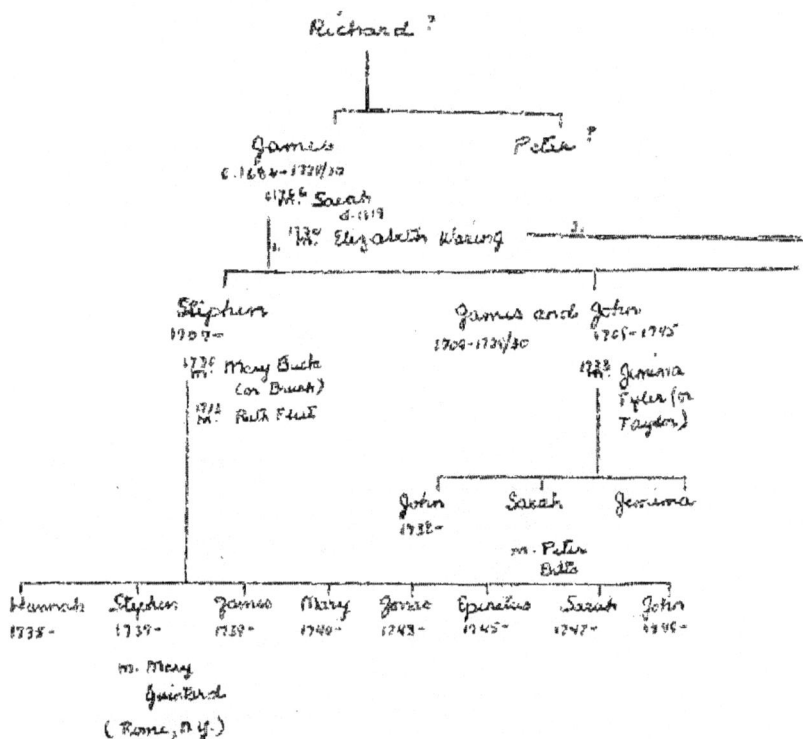

Richard?

James
c.1684-1729/30
m.1716 Sarah
d.1719
m.1723 Elizabeth Waring

Peter?

Stephen
1707-
m.1736 Mary Buck
(or Brush)
m.1711 Ruth Fleet

James and John
1709-1729/30   1705-1745
m.1733 Jemima
Tyler (or
Taylor)

John
1738-

Sarah
m. Peter
Betts

Jemima

Hannah   Stephen   James   Mary   Jonas   Epinetus   Sarah   John
1738-   1739-   1739-   1740-   1743-   1745-   1747-   1746-
          m. Mary
          Guintard
          (Rome, N.Y.)

52

The White Family

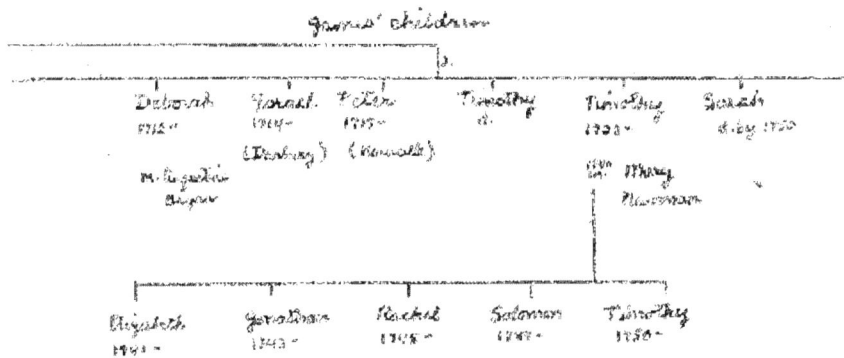

James' children
b.

Deborah	Hannah	Peter	Timothy	Timothy	Sarah
1712 -	1714 -	1715 -	d.	1720 -	d. 1720
m. Augustin	(Danbury)	(Kennett)		1749 Mary	
Brown				Newman	

Elizabeth	Jonathan	Rachel	Solomon	Timothy
1741 -	1743 -	1745 -	1747 -	1750 -

53

The White Family

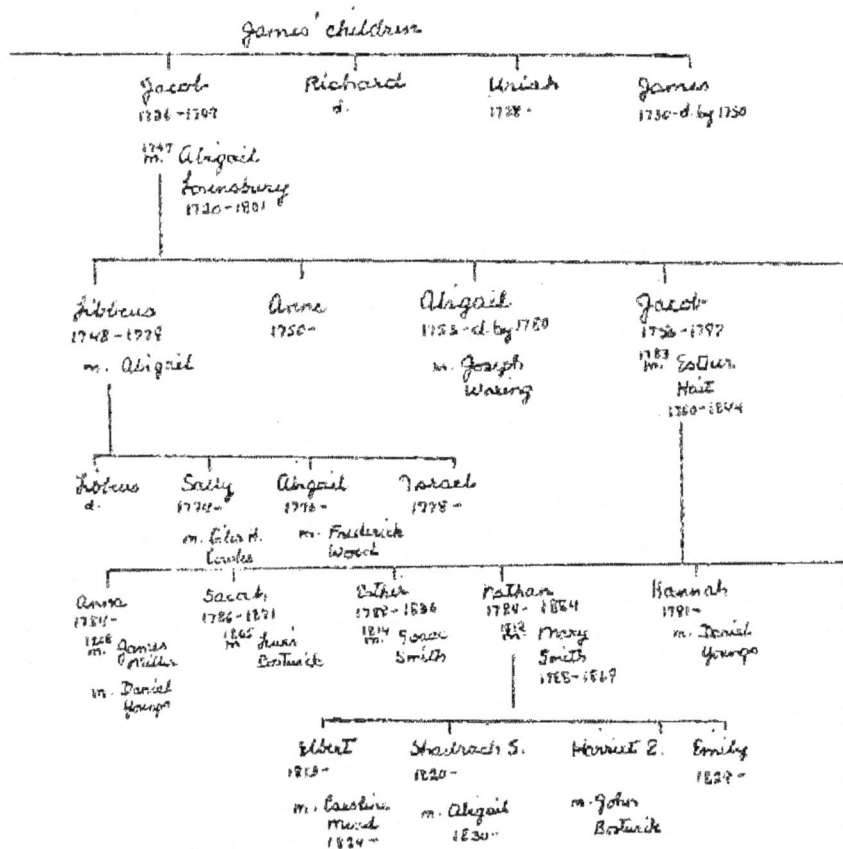

James' children

Jacob	Richard	Uriah	James
1726-1797	d.	1728-	1730-d. by 1750

1747 m. Abigail
Lownsbury
1720-1801

Libbeus	Anne	Abigail	Jacob
1748-1778	1750-	1753-d. by 1780	1756-1797
m. Abigail		m. Joseph Waring	1783 m. Esther Hait 1760-1844

Libbeus	Sally	Abigail	Israel
d.	1774-	1776-	1778-
	m. Elias H. Cowles	m. Frederick Wood	

Anna	Sarah	Esther	Nathan	Hannah
1781-	1786-1871	1788-1836	1784-1854	1791-
1808 m. James O. Miller	1805 m. Lewis Costwick	1814 m. Isaac Smith	1812 m. Mary Smith 1788-1847	m. Daniel Youngs
m. Daniel Youngs				

Elbert	Shadrach S.	Harriet E.	Emily
1818-	1820-		1824-
m. Caroline Mead 1824-	m. Abigail 1830-	m. John Bostwick	

54

The White Family

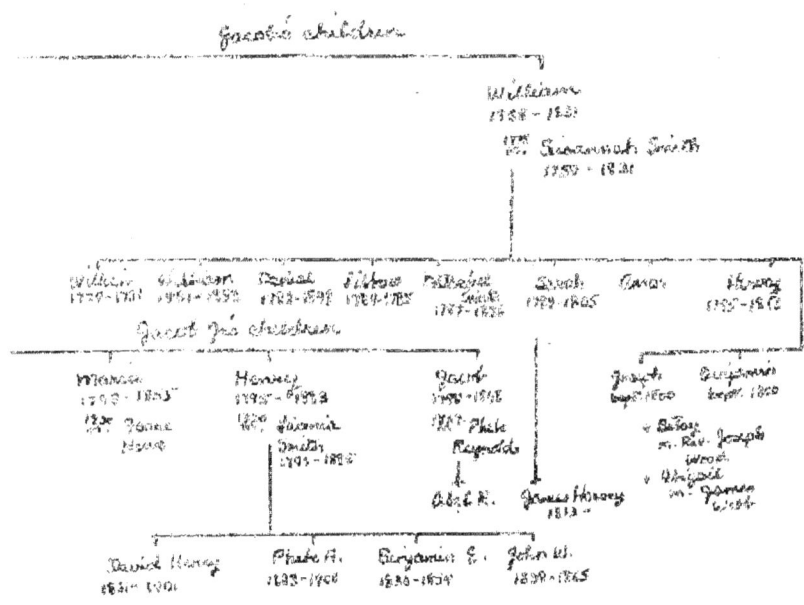

Jacob's children

William
1758 - 1833
m. Susannah Smith
1759 - 1831

William	Susannah	Daniel	Hilton	Elizabeth Smith	Jacob	Caleb	Harvey
1779-1781	1781-1859	1783-1859	1784-1785	1787-1858	1789-1865		1795-1862

Caleb Jr.'s children

Maria	Harvey	Jacob	Joseph	Benjamin
1793-1865	1795-1893	1796-1865	bapt. 1800	bapt. 1800
m. Jesse Hurd	m. Lucinda Smith 1795-1896	m. Phebe Reynolds		
		Abel R.	James Harvey 1813 -	

David Henry
1841-1901

Phebe A.	Benjamin E.	John W.
1843-1900	1838-1854	1839-1865

Footnotes

Most of the references are to the Stamford Town Records and are of three types: the land records, the town meeting records (1866 copy used), and the Probate Court records or file boxes. STR will be used for all of these, followed by the book and page reference for the land deeds; for the town meeting references TM will be used, and for the Probate Court, PC will be used.

1. Estelle F. Feinstein, Stamford from Puritan to Patriot 1641-1774, p. 103
2. Deed in showcase, Town Clerk's Office.
3. Feinstein, op. cit., p. 94
4. Jay Harris, God's Country: A History of Pound Ridge, N.Y., p. 7
5. STR, Book A, p. 450
6. Feinstein, op. cit., p. 118
7. STR, Book B, pp. 12 and 17.
8. Hurd, D. Hamilton (Compiler), History of Fairfield County, p. 720
9. STR, Book B, p. 190
10. STR, Book B, pp. 289 and 290
11. STR, Book B, pp. 58 and 291
12. STR, Book B, pp. 331, 444, 447
13. STR, Book C, p. 270
14. STR, Book B, pp. 338 and 339
15. STR, Book B, pp. 319 and 320. Mr. Robert Carder made a map of the land division, and it is very precise except for the fact that he began his measurements from what is now the New York State Line, but the line was further north in 1718. Therefore, his map is not accurate.
16. STR, Book C, p. 62
17. STR, Book E, p. 318
18. In The Whites by H. K. White it is given that James's son, James, married Elizabeth. However, the agreement with John Woren for one half of the lands to go to the subsequent children has meaning only if there are children already. Also, the land deeds from the older sons later on refer to their "younger

brothers", meaning Timothy and Jacob.

19. STR, Book C, p. 108
20. STR, TM, pp. 452, 454, 460, 478
21. STR, TM, pp. 457-458
22. STR, TM, pp. 456 and 468
23. STR, TM, pp. 459, 464, 467, 478
24. STR, PC, Vol. I, p. 60
25. Fairfield PC, Vol. I, pp. 81-82
26. STR, Book E, p. 374
27. Spencer P. Mead, _Abstract of Probate Records for the District of Stamford, County of Fairfield and State of Connecticut 1729-1802_, p. 343.
28. STR, TM, p. 484
29. STR, Book C., p. 180
30. STR, Book C, pp. 371 and 374
31. STR, Book C, p. 408 and Book D, p. 388
32. STR, Book C, p. 94 and Book D, p. 107
33. STR, Book C, p. 373 and Book D, p. 139
34. STR, Book E, p. 444
35. STR, Book D, p. 28
36. STR, Book D, p. 138
37. STR, PC, Vol. II, p. 98
38. STR, TM, pp. 479-511
39. STR, PC file box
40. STR, Book D, p. 364
41. STR, Book E, p. 403
42. STR, Book E, pp. 318 and 374
43. STR, Book E, p. 96
44. STR, TM, p. 529
45. Harris, _op. cit._, p. 15
46. STR, TM, pp. 514-544
47. STR, Book E, p. 374
48. STR, TM, pp. 547-579
49. STR, Book F, pp. 305-306
50. STR, Book F, p. 119
51. L. Raymond Waterbury, _A History of the Long Ridge Area, Pound Ridge_, p. 23
52. Tax List of 1785
53. STR, PC file box
54. STR, Book G, p. 181
55. STR, Book H, p. 359
56. STR, Book O, pp. 254 and 256
57. STR, Book H, p. 286
58. STR, Book P, p. 507
59. STR, Book G, p. 75

60. Microfilm Abstract of Greenwich, Connecticut,
    Church Records to 1850, Stanwich Church.
61. STR, TM, pp. 588-607
62. STR, TM, p. 616
63. STR, TM, p. 621
64. STR, TM, pp. 624 and 666
65. STR, TM, pp. 665-667
66. Connecticut Military Record 1775-1845, passim.
67. STR, PC file box
68. Harris, op. cit., p. 35 ff.
69. Ronald Marcus (Editor), Stamford Revolutionary
    War Damage Claims, pp. 18, 34, 36, 48, 50,
    57, 62
70. STR, PC file box
71. STR, Book K, p. 458
72. H. K. White, The Whites, p. 2
73. STR, Book I, pp. 204 and 284
74. STR, Book K. p. 547 and Book I, p. 286
75. STR, Book K, p. 396
76. STR, Book L. pp. 140 and 284
77. STR, Book N, p. 516
78. STR, Book I, p. 381 and Book N, p. 517
79. STR, Book I, pp. 311 and 242, Book K, p. 278
80. Harris, op. cit., p. 237
81. STR, Book G, p. 362, Book I, p. 116, Book I, p.
    344, Book L, p. 561, Book N, p. 626, Book M,
    p. 516, Book M, p. 536, Book M, p. 501 and
    New York Genealogical and Biographical Rec-
    ord, Vol. 55, p. 178
82. STR, TM, pp. 637, 640, 645
83. Heads of Families at the First Census of the
    United States Taken in the Year 1790 New
    York, p. 25. The number of people per fam-
    ily is given.
84. STR, Book K, p. 545
85. STR, Book N, p. 268
86. STR, PC file box
87. STR, Book N, p. 60
88. STR, Book N, p. 172 and p. 242, Book M, pp. 577
    and 578
89. STR, Book M, p. 335
90. STR, Book M. p. 31
91. Waterbury, op. cit., p. 6
92. STR, PC file box

Bibliography

Connecticut Cemeteries Fairfield County Stamford.

Connecticut Military Record 1775-1845, Hartford, Conn.
Compiled under the Authority of the General
Assembly, 1889.

Connecticut Vital Records Stamford Births, Marriages,
Deaths 1641-1852, Barbour Collection, Connecticut State Library, 1925.

Feinstein, Estelle F., Stamford from Puritan to Patriot 1641-1774, Stamford, Conn.: Stamford
Bicentennial Corp., 1976.

Harris, Jay, God's Country: A History of Pound Ridge,
N.Y., Chester, Conn.: Pequot Press, 1971.

Heads of Families at the First Census of the United
States Taken in the Year 1790 New York, Bal-
timore: Genealogical Publishing Co., Inc.,
1971.

Huntington, E. B., History of Stamford Connecticut
from Its Settlement in 1641 to the Present
Time, Including Darien, Which was One of
Its Parishes until 1820, Stamford, Conn.:
Wm. W. Gillespie and Co., 1868.

Huntington, E. B., Stamford Registration of Births,
Marriages and Deaths, Stamford, Conn.: Wm.
W. Gillespie and Co., 1874.

Huntington Town Records, Huntington, L.I.: The "Long
Islanders" Print, 1887

Hurd, D. Hamilton (Compiler), History of Fairfield
County, Connecticut, Philadelphia: J. W.
Lewis and Co., 1881

61

Marcus, Ronald (Editor), Stamford Revolutionary War
Damage Claims, Essex, Conn.: Pequot Press,
Inc. 1968

Mead, Spencer P., Abstract of Church Records of the
Town of Stamford, County of Fairfield and
State of Connecticut from the earliest rec-
ords extant to 1850, 1924.

Mead, Spencer P., Abstract of Probate Records for the
District of Stamford, County of Fairfield
and State of Connecticut 1729-1802.

New York Genealogical and Biographical Record, New
York: New York Genealogical and Biographical Record, Vols. 1-106, 1870-1975

The Stamford Town Records: the Land Records, the
Town Meeting Records 1630-1806, and the Probate Court Records.

The Eighteenth-Century Tax Lists of Stamford

Waterbury, L. Raymond, A History of the Long Ridge
Area, Pound Ridge, June 1972.

White, H. K., The Whites, 1906

Microfilm:

Abstract of Greenwich, Connecticut, Church Records to
1850.

Abstract of Records and Tombstones of the Town of
Greenwich.

1800 Census for Fairfield and Hartford Counties.

Colonial Families of Long Island, New York, and Connecticut, (Herbert Silversmith Collection).

Eardeley Manuscript.

www.ingramcontent.com/pod-product-compliance
Lightning Source LLC
Chambersburg PA
CBHW070915270326
41927CB00011B/2583